ISAIAH AND HIS INTERPRETERS

**by
John J. Schmitt**

PAULIST PRESS
New York/Mahwah

Library of Congress Cataloging-in-Publication Data

Schmitt, John J.
    Isaiah and his interpreters.

    Includes bibliographies and index.
    1. Bible. O.T. Isaiah—Criticism, interpretation, etc. 2. Bible. O.T. Isaiah—Criticism, interpretation, etc.—History. I. Title.
BS1515.2.S38   1986   224'.106   86-9311
ISBN 0-8091-2826-8 (pbk.)

Published by Paulist Press
997 Macarthur Boulevard
Mahwah, N.J. 07430

Printed and bound in the United States of America

Contents

To
Frances J. Schmitt
my mother
on her eightieth birthday, December 6, 1985

and in memoriam
Silvester J. Schmitt
my father
† February 9, 1964

Table of Abbreviations

AB	Anchor Bible
AnBib	Analecta Biblica
AO	Analecta Orientalia
art. cit.	articulo citato (= in the cited article)
AThANT	Abhandlungen zur Theologie des Alten und Neuen Testaments
BCE	Before the Common Era
BETL	Biblotheca Ephemeridum Theologicarum Lovaniensium
BK	Biblischer Kommentar
BZAW	Beihefte zur Zeitschrift für die alttestamentliche Wissenschaft
c.	circa (= about)
ca.	circa (= about)
CBQ	*Catholic Biblical Quarterly*
CBQMS	Catholic Biblical Quarterly Monograph Series
C.C.S.L.	Corpus Christianorum, Series Latina
cf.	confer (= compare)
cols.	columns
DS	*Dictionnaire de la Spiritualité*
e.g.	exempli gratia (= for example)
et al.	et alii (= and others)
ETL	*Ephemerides Theologicae Lovanienses*
FS	Festschrift (= essays in honor of)
HTR	*Harvard Theological Review*
ibid.	ibidem (= in the same place)
i.e.	id est (= that is)
IOVCB	Interpreter's One-Volume Commentary on the Bible

JBL	*Journal of Biblical Literature*
JSOT	*Journal for the Study of the Old Testament*
JSOTSS	JSOT Supplement Series
KJV	King James Version
n.	note
NCB	New Century Bible
NCE	*New Catholic Encyclopedia*
n.d.	no date
NEB	New English Bible
OT	Old Testament
OTL	Old Testament Library
op. cit.	opere citato (= in the cited work)
p.	page
pb	paperback
PG	Migne Patrologie, Graeca
pp.	pages
repr.	reprinted
rev.	revised
RSV	Revised Standard Version
SBLDS	Society of Biblical Literature Dissertation Series
SBT	Studies in Biblical Theology
SJT	*Scottish Journal of Theology*
SVT	*Supplements to Vetus Testamentum*
TBP	Torch Bible Paperback
TLZ	*Theologische Literaturzeitung*
TZ	*Theologische Zeitschrift*
v	verse
vol.	volume
vols.	volumes
vs.	versus
VT	*Vetus Testamentum*
vv	verses
WMANT	Wissenschaftliche Monographien zum Alten und Neuen Testament
ZAW	*Zeitschrift für die alttestamentliche Wissenschaft*
ZTK	*Zeitschrift für Theologie und Kirche*

1.

Isaiah and the Bible

The Hebrew Bible/Old Testament is a record of the dialogue between God and Ancient Israel.

God speaks in many ways, and the means we have to hear that voice differ. God spoke to the people of Ancient Israel through the prophets sent to them and also spoke within the hearts of individual Israelites. Believers throughout the ages have been aware of various ways in which God speaks: through leaders who are specially sent by God, through the words and actions of the prophets recorded in the Bible, and within the heart of each human being. God speaks to us today in a similar variety. God speaks through the Bible, through the community and its leaders, and within the hearts of persons open to the Spirit of God.

Scripture has always been a place where the believing communities and the individual could hear the voice of God. Both Jews and Christians have always been convinced of this. The Bible is not just the record of the past but also a means of reaching God in the present. Admittedly, in certain times and settings, the Bible has not been allowed to speak for itself. It might be said that this was especially true in the Middle Ages when the Bible remained in Latin and religious people learned the Bible and its story of God's love for us mostly from preachers and from the art of the churches and cathedrals.

With the Reformation, more Christians had access to the Bible itself. The popular use of the Bible grew because the leaders of the Reformation encouraged Christians to read the Bible and also enabled them to do so by translating the Bible into the language that people spoke, the vernacular.

Within the Roman Catholic church, Bible reading has taken a most dramatic turn in the twentieth century. The twentieth century popes were preceded by Leo XIII, who, in his encyclical *Providentissimus Deus* in 1893, encouraged all to read the Bible daily. Pope Pius XII in 1943 both freed Catholic biblical scholarship from the cloud of suspicion it was under and exhorted all Catholics to read the Bible in the spirit and with the Spirit in which and through which it was written.

Today, more Christians read the Bible than ever before. Bible study groups have appeared in heartening numbers, even among Catholics. This development is clearly the result of the Spirit moving within the churches, evident especially in the encouragement that the hierarchy continues to give to the study and praying of Scripture.

Isaiah as Central to the Bible

This book focuses on one book of the Bible for a special kind of analysis. It takes the book of Isaiah and attempts to see the man whom God had chosen as a special spokesman in critical times in the history of God's people in the Old Testament. The closer one looks, the more there is to see. Scholars have peered at this man and his thoughts through various kinds of glasses. You might say that how the glass was ground showed differing understandings of this prophet. The following review of those different depictions of Isaiah and the ways that scholars have come to make their assessments of him will help the reader see the richness and diversity within the book of Isaiah.

Isaiah stands out in the Bible in many ways. Some of those ways appear in the first chapter of this book. But already here we might mention some other distinctive features of Isaiah. In the next pages, we will see how the themes of Isaiah are central to the thought of the Bible as a whole and especially representative of the Old Testament. Isaiah is not only an essential part of the Bible but also belongs to its essence—he points to the heart of the biblical message.

One might—just for fun—show this centrality visually. When you open a copy of the Bible just about in the middle, the center will probably be the beginning of the book of Isaiah. (At least this is my experience with the *Good News Bible* because, while there are 1448 pages in the edition that I have, Isaiah begins on page 742, at almost the exact center.) But the words of Isaiah are far more central than any such physical measurement.

The chapters of this book approach the prophet Isaiah with various questions and from various perspectives. These different questions and perspectives complement each other because they display the various facets of the precious gem, the book of Isaiah. When we turn the gem, we see the light reflected in different angles and see the various colors that are released. Even the color and light from the area around the gem are heightened and accentuated by the brilliant and many-splendored jewel. To analyze the book of Isaiah is to find treasure of incredible value and attraction.

The realization that God used human language to express the divine should influence the reading and study of the Bible. In choosing Ancient Israel as partner in conversation in antiquity, God decided, in a way, for this revelation to be limited by the time period and setting and circumstances of ancient Israel's existence. Thus, the language we call Biblical Hebrew is the language that the inspired spokesmen of God in the Bible usually used. Anyone wanting to get close to Isaiah will have to watch that prophet's words and use of language. God chose this language for the witness to the divine in ancient Israel, and we today are compelled to follow the lead of God in this matter.

Ancient texts present the wisdom that the past has handed down to succeeding generations. Although the Christian looks at the Bible in more ways than this bald statement would indicate, one should at times see the Bible in this light. In biblical studies, the word "wisdom" refers to certain forms of speech and categories of thought that Israel shared with other cultures of the ancient Near East. The Bible contains three books that most scholars classify as wisdom literature: Job, Proverbs and Ecclesiastes. Isaiah includes a number of passages that possess wisdom characteristics, but the book cannot be called wisdom literature. One must say, though, that parts of it are strongly influenced by that outlook and share that style.

Some people see the whole Old Testament as the place where God basically scolds the people and tells what will happen if they do not behave. This image of God, of course, derives from only certain passages of the Old Testament. (One can find the same kind of passages in the New Testament.) The reality is that the eighth century prophets had to scold and warn. Isaiah played that role well. On this point one might say that Isaiah could represent the aspect of threat and punishment in the Old Testament.

Many passages of the Hebrew Bible narrate how the prophets of ancient Israel called out to the people to turn back to God. Israel is frequently depicted as being unfaithful. God is often portrayed as sending spokesmen to call Israel to repentance and conversion. Isaiah surely does this too, and does it well. This call to conversion not only is representative of the Old Testament/Hebrew Bible, but also flows over into Jesus's preliminary requirement for his followers.

The Old Testament is the record of God working with humankind to form a society, a means of association with God. This linking of God with the human community and enterprise is called by the Hebrew Bible the covenant. Covenant appears in many forms in the Old Testament. There is the covenant with Noah, then the covenant with Abraham, and the covenant through Moses, as well as the covenant with David, to mention just the major ones. (Note how Paul in Romans 9:4 uses the plural "covenants.") Just as does the whole Hebrew Bible, Isaiah exhibits a preoccupation with the relationship between Israel and its God, a relationship often described as a covenant.

The Bible is the witness to God's promises. The promises of God include many things. Basic among these promises is that God will be Israel's own God and they will be the people of this God alone. But God also promises the time of fulfillment and the means to that fulfillment. The promises in Isaiah fit in well with those already mentioned. The time of forgiveness and cure, the time of wholeness and happiness, the new leader to usher in those times—the pages of Isaiah are filled with the hope and promise of all that the human heart can long for. Isaiah must be seen as preeminent among the books of promise in the Bible.

It is clear that the God of Israel demands holiness and purity. What is sullied or tarnished must be cleansed. Where service of God is corrupted, there must be a purification. The whole Old Testament and the New Testament proclaim this requirement. God has loved a people that has strayed, the prophets say, and God must make them clean by a process of purification and cleansing. Isaiah preaches this with a special intensity. In this he can be seen as central to the message of the whole Bible.

All these different facets of the book of the prophet Isaiah have held certain scholars captive in their power to attract. In the following chapters we will see how each can be taken as the major thrust of the teaching of the prophet.

The book of Isaiah in a way represents the totality of the Bible. Creation, the start of God's work, is found nowhere else more frequently in the Bible than in Isaiah 40–55. And the final struggle between the forces of God and the forces of evil is found with a unique focus in Isaiah 24–27 and in other apocalyptic passages in Isaiah. Views of both the beginning and the end are found in Isaiah. Not many other books of the Bible make that claim.

Isaiah Awaits Us

To investigate Isaiah, then, is to look into central ideas and themes of the Bible. But the prophet Isaiah himself stands at a particularly critical time in Israel's history. The two kingdoms into which Solomon's realm had split were prospering as never before. War loomed in the immediate future. Isaiah is the only prophet we know who clearly refers to both the destruction of the northern kingdom in 722 and the terrifying and potentially fatal attack against the southern kingdom in 701. Isaiah stood at a most challenging time in Israel's history. Many ears turned to him in that day.

Many eyes ought to turn to him in these days of social upheaval and nuclear threat. Surely our century has come to times just as critical for it as were Isaiah's times for Israel. History will not come this way again. It is no surprise that people are turning to the Bible in this time of crisis.

The need is to read the Bible correctly. There have always been different interpretations of the Bible in general. It is no surprise then that Isaiah gets different treatment from different scholars. This book will discuss those scholars whose interpretations of Isaiah have found a serious reception in the scholarly world. Interpretations from the purely economic or sociological order have not been included.

This book will serve the average Bible reader as an introduction to the book of Isaiah and to his place in the biblical tradition. It offers details and perspectives to the student who wants to know more about Isaiah than a standard introduction to the Bible offers. It may serve the specialist in recalling or pointing out discussions that have so far occurred only in scholarly circles. Most of all, it is an invitation to read the book of Isaiah and to look behind the book to see the man whose very name means "Yahweh saves."

2.

The Question of Isaiah

Isaiah is the longest book of the Bible when one counts the chapters, although the book of Jeremiah does have more words. Isaiah is also distinguished by being the prophetic book most frequently quoted in the New Testament and cited in the Jewish Mishnah. And among the group of Jewish sectarians who produced the Dead Sea Scrolls, Isaiah was the most copied prophetic book.[1]

Isaiah has always had a particular attraction for Christians because of its use in the presentation of Jesus as Messiah. Jesus himself read Isaiah 61:1–2 aloud in the synagogue:

> The Spirit of the Lord is upon me,
> because he has anointed me to preach good news to the
>   poor
> He has sent me to proclaim release to the captives
> and recovering of sight to the blind,
> to set at liberty those who are oppressed
> to proclaim the acceptable year of the Lord.
>
> Luke 4:17–21

Acts shows Philip applying Isaiah 53 to the death and resurrection of Jesus (Acts 8:26–35). The early chapters of Isaiah bear their own witness to Christ, according to some readers. The words about Immanuel (7:14, 8:8, 10), the son born to us (9:6), the removal of sin (1:18, 6:7), the waters of salvation (12:3)—all have spoken to Christians across the ages of the person and work of the redeemer.

The New Testament itself encourages its readers to look to the prophet Isaiah. Paul, the earliest New Testament writer, quotes Isaiah nineteen times, five times giving the name of Isaiah.[2] Luke makes use of Isaiah more than any other writer in the New Testament.[3] John is so bold as to say that Isaiah "saw the glory" of Jesus (John 12:41).[4] Some writers have been so enthusiastic about Isaiah as to call him the fifth evangelist.[5]

The popularity and influence of Isaiah's book is striking. Certainly the man who stands behind that book is worthy of investigation. From very early times most people thought that all sixty-six chapters contained only words that came directly from the eighth-century citizen of Jerusalem, but even in the first century there were signs that not everything was that clear cut. The question of Isaiah—and which words are his—inevitably arose.

Attribution to Isaiah

The gospel according to Mark (Mark 1:2) claims to be quoting Isaiah when it invokes these words: "Behold, I send my messenger before thy face, who shall prepare thy way." This quotation is from the book of Malachi, and even if the next line is indeed a quotation from Isaiah:

The voice of one crying in the wilderness:
  "Prepare the way of the Lord,
  make his paths straight—"

Mark 1:3

nevertheless, it seems that the author of Mark attributed to Isaiah words that had not been his before.

One individual from the eleventh century voiced hesitation whether the whole book of Isaiah came from just one person in the times of Kings Uzziah, Ahaz, and Hezekiah. Ibn Ezra, a Jewish commentator, pointed out the difficulty he had seeing Isaiah speak directly to people who would live a century and a half after him. At the time, not many scholars shared his misgivings. It took six centuries for those misgivings to become the majority position among scholars. The next chapter outlines that process.

Current biblical scholarship regularly warns against simply equating the words contained in a prophet's book with the words as spoken by the prophet himself. Scholars now understand that the books of the Old Testament grew over a period of many years.

To begin, it is not always clear whether the prophet himself was the one to write down his words or whether some person close to him began the collection of his sayings and passed them on to later generations.

Spoken Word

How the words of the prophets survived has been a major debate in biblical studies.[6] German scholarship was first to stress the oral transmission of the materials in the Bible before they were written down.[7] Hermann Gunkel was the first of a succession of scholars who proposed that many parts of the Bible had been passed on without a written text.[8] The battle over the significance of oral tradition waged most heatedly in Swedish scholarship.[9] The oral delivery of a story and oral repetitions of the utterances of an important speaker were central social and religious events in the life of simple and idyllic Israel.

This idea of the orality of the biblical materials finds obvious application to the prophetic texts. Isaiah, after all, was a preacher, not a writer. The prophets in general are never depicted as scholars, scribes, or writers. The Bible introduces prophetic words not with "This is what the prophet wrote," but with "The words which he saw" or what he said when "the word of the Lord came to him." Twice Isaiah is told to write something, yet what he writes may be no more than three or four words.[10] Jeremiah dictates many words to a man who seems to serve as his secretary, but he himself is not depicted as taking pen in hand.[11] Ezekiel sees a scroll and eats it, but never puts his own words on it.[12]

Written Word

Thus, the prophetic texts themselves and their own ambiguity allow for and even seem to encourage the debate concerning the formation of the first collections of the words of the prophets.

There are some who say that the words of the prophets were recorded very soon after they were spoken, and those who make that claim point to the antiquity of the written word in the ancient world. Several centuries ago a popular idea was that writing came late in the history of the human race, or at least late in the history of ancient Israel. Moses could not have written the Pentateuch, the argument went, because writing had not yet been invented. But as scholarship progressed, many texts and documents from ancient times were discovered and deciphered, and these show that the written word goes back at least to 3000 BCE.

The original writing of the prophetic texts cannot be determined simply on the basis of the antiquity of writing in human society. In any event, writing in the ancient world and in ancient Israel began at a very early time. In the ancient Near East, writing often existed along with the need of the spoken word: messengers from one king going to another court in which the messenger is to deliver the message orally often carried the written message as well, the written form serving as a check against the spoken word.[13]

Even so, some scholars find it unlikely that the prophet was the first to put his own words into writing. The prophet usually appears concerned to convey his message to his contemporaries, rather than to preserve it for posterity. His message warned and confronted his own generation. It was his disciples, the circle who surrounded the prophet because his words moved them, that reduced his words to writing. What was the occasion for this initial writing? Perhaps it was the death of the prophet. Or it could have been a significant political event that seemed related to certain words of the prophet. These written words, then, began the process of forming the prophetic book.

Additional Words

In antiquity, the saying goes, every new copy of a book was a new edition.[14] The person who copied the work would add, modify, and update. Errors were corrected, unclear statements clarified, and style modified. The copyist, more an editor than a secretary, would revise the work on the basis of personal insights and new political developments, or would add interpretations to meet new demands in society. There is no reason to project the more recent concept of exact transference of an individual's words from one generation to the next by some indelible record back into the society of ancient Israel.

Thus, the name of a new political enemy might be inserted in an older text to bring its application up to date.[15] New religious or political policies would call for an adaptation of the older text to the new situation. Previously ambiguous figures in the text would be identified as someone from the contemporary scene. Innumerable other kinds of clarification could occur.

Another way prophetic books likely grew is through the creation of quite new material. A prophet's words may not have been numerous or long enough to stand by themselves, lending themselves easily to being combined with already collected sayings. The resulting work, actually a collection from perhaps several different authors, including the editor or redactor, might form a unity which only the skillfully trained ear and the sharp eye could distinguish.

The idea that a text could be increased and modified in order to gain clarity and to remove ambiguity seems clear enough from observable developments in the ancient transmission of the biblical materials. The tendency to add clarification and even to rearrange large sections of the prophetic sayings can be seen in the Greek version of the book of Jeremiah. The translator saw the appropriateness of a different arrangement and did not hesitate to move what is now called Jer 46–51 from its place at the end of the collection to right after Jer 25:12–13 where Yahweh says,

> I will punish the king of Babylon and that nation, the land of the Chaldeans, for their iniquity . . . I will bring upon that land all the words which I have uttered against it, everything written in this book . . .

This rearrangement allowed for clearer reading and brought these prophetic words more in line with similar prophetic collections. These collections usually had this arrangement: threats against one's own people, threats against other peoples and, then, promises of restoration. Obviously finding the original words and the original intention of the writer or speaker of the biblical prophetic words is a complicated task.

Dating Texts

Three different clues have been left in the biblical text which help to locate the different writers or speakers. (1) Since the Hebrew Bible was written over a period of about one thousand years, one can expect to find different styles of writing, both in the choice of words and in the selection of other ways to express human thought in linguistic forms. Just as the English of Chaucer differs from that of Ernest Hemingway, so, ideally, the Hebrew of Moses would differ from that of a person living at the time of exile in Babylonia. (2) Many scholars also think that Israel's religious and intellectual life progressed through various stages and had a variety of developments. Thus, attacks on the making of idols may well be dated to a period after the time when idol making was first condemned. (3) Finally, each text reflects the historical situation at the time of composition. For example, when the name of Cyrus appears in Isaiah 44 and 45:

> I am the Lord . . . who says of Cyrus, "He is my shepherd, and he shall fulfill all my purpose . . ."
>
> Isa 44:24, 28

> Thus says the Lord to his anointed, to Cyrus,
>   whose right hand I have grasped,
> to subdue nations before him
>   and ungird the loins of kings,
> to open doors before him
>   that gates may not be closed.
>
> Isa 45:1

many scholars argue that this name would not occur in texts written before that man was alive.

The later meaning of a text is influenced by what it was originally meant to say. Most theologians today feel that knowing something about the historical setting of a text aids in determining the original meaning of the text and also in appropriating that text in one's own faith life.

Thus many scholars throughout history, but especially in the last two centuries, have sought to discover when and in what settings particular words were first spoken or written. This search has led to many debates and to lively discussions, as the next chapter will show. The application of each of these three criteria for dating specific texts is not a mathematical science. Accordingly, the certainty of a particular analysis of a biblical text is somewhat like the conviction one has about one's personal understanding of the meaning of any great literary work.

These questions require far more consideration for a total presentation, and a full discussion would fill many volumes. We will be satisfied with raising those questions and with offering here, in summary form, the generally discussed results of the scientific study of the book of Isaiah in the past two centuries. Specific scholars and their analyses are reviewed in the following chapter.

Sections of Isaiah

Primary among such conclusions is the difference between Isa 1–39 and Isa 40–66. This is a distinction that was hinted at already in the Middle Ages by Ibn Ezra. It was proposed in Christian scholarship in the eighteenth century, and, from about the middle of the nineteenth century on, most critical scholars have called Isa 1–39 "First Isaiah" and Isa 40–66 "Second Isaiah."

One might note here in passing the difference in the use of terminology between First and Second Isaiah on the one hand and First and Second Samuel on the other, or even First and Second Timothy. First Isaiah is the prophet of Jerusalem; Second Isaiah is the anonymous prophet in the exile whose words begin in chapter 40 of the same book as First Isaiah. First and Second Samuel are two books that were originally one book. First and

Second Timothy are two books literarily addressed to the same person.

A major modification of this two-prophet theory about the book of Isaiah occurred in the final years of the nineteenth century. The proposal was that Isa 40–55 is different enough from Isa 56–66 to warrant the designation "Third Isaiah" for the last eleven chapters. Thus, first Isaiah preached in Jerusalem in the eighth century BCE. Second Isaiah prophesied in the exile of the sixth century BCE. Third Isaiah is material which comes from the time of the return to Jerusalem after the exile and reflects the struggles of the period of restoration in the fifth century BCE.

So, to find the sayings of Isaiah of eighth-century Jerusalem, a scholar goes to Isa 1–39. But the search only begins there. All the criteria of finding the real words of the prophet still apply. As with all the prophetic books, so with Isaiah: there must have been an early collection or two, some editing, some explanations, additional clarifications, applications and elaborations.

Since many things happened in Israel after the eighth century, the book could well have gone through redactions and editions in order to bring it up to date or even to bring it in line with current-day thinking and with the events which formed the milieu of the people of God at that time.

This process of expansion by clarification could last until the text became regarded as so sacred that it could not be modified in any way. In the book of Deuteronomy, one can see this development appearing in the text itself:

> You shall not add to the word which I command you, nor take from it.
>
> Deut 4:2

> Everything that I command you you shall be careful to do; you shall not add to it or take from it.
>
> Deut 12:32

In Isaiah there is no such statement. Many scholars judge that modifications may have been made as late as the second century BCE. It could be no later than this, for the Greek translation was probably made during that century, and the earliest copy of Isaiah found among the Dead Sea Scrolls comes also from about that time.

Much work has been done in sorting out the authentic sayings of Isaiah. Some chapters in 1–39 are clearly not from eighth-century Isaiah. The easiest to identify is the section Isa 24–27 which has enough differences and peculiarities that a consensus has formed that it is not Isaiah.

Another section not likely from the original Isaiah is chapters 36–39. These are narratives that have been borrowed from the books of Kings in order to bring all the material about the prophet Isaiah together in one place. Although these narratives may give some accurate information about Isaiah not contained in chapters 1–23 and 28–35, many scholars see a different image of Isaiah in this section.

Chapters 13–22 and 33–35 are generally viewed as too mixed to make broad statements about the authentic nature of their contents. Some scholars, however, see parts of chapters 14, 17, 19, 22 and 33 as reflecting the preaching of Isaiah, but there is no large agreement among scholars on these.

The authentic words of Isaiah usually stand out by their power and vividness. Isaiah conveyed his message in concrete and specific words. Many scholars consider him among the greatest poets of the Bible, for his images and comparisons are visual and striking. His style is compact and forceful. His prophecies form artistic wholes. He has earned the praises he has received as an original and powerful preacher. This is the spokesman of God scholars identify in the book of Isaiah.

Notes

1. One can add that the process of translating Isaiah into Aramaic may have begun already in the time of Jesus. This Aramaic translation (Targum) of Isaiah might have influenced the thought and language of Jesus and the early Christian community. The Aramaic translation of Isaiah seems to have influenced the Aramaic translations of several of the other prophets as well. See Bruce D. Chilton, *The Glory of Israel: The Theology and Pro-*

venience of the Isaiah Targum (JSOTSS 23; Sheffield: JSOT, 1983).

2. Rom 9:27, 29; 10:16, 20; 15:12. See the handy *Old Testament Quotations in the New Testament* (Helps for Translators; New York: American Bible Society, 1980).

3. James A. Sanders, "Isaiah in Luke," *Interpretation* 36 (1982) 144–55.

4. John and Isaiah both emphasize faith; see G. Segala, "La fede come opzione fondamentale in Isaia e Giovanni," *Studia Patavina* 15 (1968) 355–81.

5. "Isaias has so many prophecies concerning the King and the kingdom that out of his sixty-six chapters a fifth Gospel can be composed," William J. McGarry, *He Cometh* (New York: America, 1947) 133. (Older Catholic books on Scripture spell "Isaiah" as "Isaias," because the latter derives from the Latin, and that form was preferred by Catholics until the 1960's.) Eusebius, a scholar of the fourth century, put it this way: "One ought to say, too, that Isaiah is an evangelist, because he performed the same service as the evangelists. For he proclaims the Son of God in different ways: sometimes he speaks of him as God, sometimes he prophesies his entry into heaven and predicts the birth of Emmanuel from a virgin, and his resurrection. One ought also to say that he is an apostle, for his book demonstrates this when it says: 'And the Lord said, Whom shall I send, and who will go to this people? And he said, Behold, here I am; send me.' " Eusebius of Caesarea, *Der Jesajakommentar* (ed. Joseph Ziegler; Berlin: Akademie, 1975) 3–4 (in the section on Isaiah 1:1). (I thank Rev. Joseph T. Lienhard, S.J., for suggestions with this translation.)

6. Scholars first saw that the Pentateuchal materials were passed on orally prior to being written down before they saw that the same idea of oral transmission should be used in understanding the prophetic books. Thus, already in 1554, Calvin described Moses as writing down the previous oral tradition, lest it become corrupted over the coming generations. See Douglas A. Knight, *Rediscovering the Traditions of Israel* (2d ed; SBLDS; Missoula: Scholars Press, 1975) 41. Knight also discusses the French priest, Richard Simon (1638–1712), who had earlier emphasized tradition, but more a written tradition than an oral one, pp. 48–51.

7. Hans Schmidt and Hugo Gressmann were collaborators with Hermann Gunkel in this approach.

8. Gunkel stressed that the eighth century prophets spoke only short sayings in traditional forms. Thus Isaiah never really produced a coherent collection of sayings. For Gunkel, Ezekiel was the first prophet to write a book. See Ronald E. Clements, *One Hundred Years of Old Testament Interpretation* (Philadelphia: Westminster, 1976) 58.

9. Knight (see n. 4 above) traces in detail the Scandinavian debate on the whole traditio-historical question, pp. 215–399.

10. In Isa 8:1 the command is to write *lemaher šallal haš baz* ("Belonging to Maher-shalal-hash-baz," RSV). In Isa 30:8, what is to be written is not as clear. It might be the words of accusation in vv 9–11 or even vv 9–14. But far more likely it refers to the phrase "Rahab who sits still" (*rahab hem šabet*), indicating that Egypt is not to be feared.

11. Jer 36:4

12. Ezek 2:8–3:3

13. See G. W. Ahlström, "Oral and Written Transmission: Some Considerations," *HTR* 59 (1966) 69–81, esp. 75–76.

14. Perhaps even the idea of "book" is anachronistic. Cf. the development of the Gilgamesh story in Jeffrey Tigay, *The Evolution of the Gilgamesh Epic* (Philadelphia: University of Pennsylvania, 1982). It took over a millennium for the text to become somewhat stabilized.

15. For example, Peter R. Ackroyd ("The Book of Isaiah," *IOVCB*, 341) sees Isaiah 13 and 14 as originally general descriptions of the day of Yahweh (perhaps chapter 14 referring specifically to Assyria) but which were later applied to Babylon by the insertion of that name.

3.

First Isaiah

The book of Isaiah became the touchstone of scholarly ortho-doxy as soon as critical scholars were convinced of the existence of a second Isaiah. But scholars had begun very slowly to propose that view and to debate whether there could be a division in the book of Isaiah between the sayings from the real Isaiah of the eighth century and the words from speakers and writers of later times. Those suspicions, proposals, and debates became frequent in the nineteenth century. Tracing that story can bring out the peculiarity of Isaiah, and it can help identify and underline those things that set off the "second Isaiah" from First Isaiah.

Early Evidence

Although the Middle Ages are usually given as the time when scholars first questioned whether Isaiah would have addressed the exiles who were to live in Babylon two centuries later, there is a kind of evidence from an earlier era of a surprising division within the book of Isaiah. That evidence comes from the Dead Sea Scrolls.

The "Dead Sea Scrolls" is the name given to the writings that were discovered deep in caves that overlook the Dead Sea from a northern area of its western shore.[1] These scrolls are of three kinds, according to the material they contain: biblical texts, non-biblical texts that were already known, and other writings that had not been known before. The writings of this third category were probably composed by the group of dissident Jews of the second or first century before the Common Era, who had hidden this library as they were preparing to flee their desert settlement for time.

Two different copies of the book of Isaiah were found among the Scrolls. The older text contains almost the whole book of Isaiah. This older text (early first century BCE) has a curious separation in the middle of its scroll. At that time, the books of the Bible were not divided into numbered chapters or verses. Even without the advantage of numbered chapters, the older Isaiah text makes a clear break between our chapters 33 and 34, leaving two lines completely blank.

This kind of division is not encountered anywhere else among the scrolls.[2] Presumably the scribe or copyist thought that these were two different works, and that this distinction should be indicated and preserved on the copy being made. Even if this division does not reveal why the scribe made the break, it is not by chance that it was made exactly where a new style takes over. Indeed, after a series of woes (28:1, 29:1 [also "Woe" in Hebrew], 30:1, 31:1, 33:1) the call to the nations is striking:

Draw near, O nations, to hear
 and hearken, O peoples!
Let the earth listen, and all that fills it;
 the world, and all that comes from it.

Isa 34:1

Early Church and Rabbinic Period

Beyond this small piece of evidence, there seems to have been no recorded case for many generations when someone thought that the book of Isaiah represented the work of more than one person. Although several scholars of the Christian church wrote commentaries on Isaiah and although the Jewish scholars of the Mishnaic and Talmudic times praised Isaiah as one of the greatest religious leaders, no one seems to have given his work the critical attention that results in theories of multiple authorship. Such theories developed later and have now become standard assumptions in contemporary scholarship.

Origen, the earliest great Christian scholar (185–254), wrote the first known commentary on the book of Isaiah.[3] Although Origen did not complete this commentary, it seems to have influenced later interpretation, especially, for example, Eusebius, who relied on Origen heavily in his own study of and commentary on Isaiah. Origen is distinctive for, among other things, his consultation with Jews for their understanding of the Scriptures.[4] But usually his interpretation is so allegorical,[5] that the question of whether an eighth century prophet would directly address readers of the sixth century did not occur to Origen.

Eusebius of Caesarea (265–340) wrote his commentary on Isaiah rather late in his life.[6] Eusebius was at heart a biblical scholar, and only pressing administrative duties frustrated his desire to devote himself more fully to scriptural study. His later years must have been satisfying, for then he wrote his commentaries on Isaiah and the Psalms. Much of Eusebius's philosophical and theological thought follows that of Origen, but in his scripture study, Eusebius is less given to allegorical interpretation than is Origen.[7]

Even so, for all his attention to historical matters, Eusebius does not dream of multiple authorship for Isaiah. Whenever any difficulty arises, he feels quite happy to invoke some spiritual interpretation rather than to face the kinds of questions that modern scholars regularly ask. As far as he was concerned, Isaiah wrote the whole book.

The only Latin father to write a commentary on Isaiah that has survived is Jerome (342–430).[8] Jerome's commentary is quite original and fresh, with good theological reflection and attention to philological problems.[9]

On the particular point of the difference between 1–39 and 40–66, Jerome has no bold proposal to make. Despite Jerome's general insistence on historical interpretation, he sees the people who are to be consoled in chapter 40 as "not just Israel and Jacob and Judah" but many peoples who have become the people of God.[10] This statement does not seem to reflect the eighth century BCE but rather Christian experience. Even when commenting on Isaiah's mention of Cyrus (44:28; 45:1), rather than asking who wrote the words, Jerome is more concerned to point out that the prophecy of Isaiah about Cyrus finds fulfillment in the Greek writer Xenophon, when he narrates Cyrus's victories.[11]

Jerome wrote his commentary on Isaiah with the commentary of Eusebius before him. Some scholars have claimed that Jerome simply borrowed from Eusebius for much of his interpretation. This is certainly an exaggeration.[12] Jerome has his own insights. But although Jerome knew Hebrew and the Bible well, his historical imagination did not lead him to conceive of two Isaiahs.

Other scholars of the early church who wrote commentaries on Isaiah that survive in Greek include Ephrem the Syrian (306–373),[13] Pseudo-Basil (c. 330–379), John Chrysostom (344–407),[14] Cyril of Alexandria (c. 370–444)[15] and Theodoret of Cyrrhus (393–458).[16]

The rabbis who appear in the Talmud (published c. 500) had a particular attraction to and affection for Isaiah. Various legends about his martyrdom had already developed in the early rabbinic period.[17] Some rabbis claimed that Isaiah was second in greatness only to Moses, for Isaiah had reduced the whole of Torah to six commandments.[18]

The Talmud does not really pose the question of dividing the book of Isaiah in two parts. Yet the rabbis indeed recognize that Isaiah alone did not write the book. They say that the book of Isaiah was written by Isaiah and the men of Hezekiah.[19] It is likely that the phrase "the men of Hezekiah" refers to the appearance of that phrase in Prov 25:1, where these men are responsible for one of the collections within the book of Proverbs. Nevertheless, this is a kind of critical reflection by scholars of the early centuries of the Common Era which finds multiple authorship in Isaiah.

Medieval Period

Ibn Ezra has been called "the first Jewish Bible critic."[20] His commentary on Isaiah does not really set out to prove any theory about the book of Isaiah. But he does raise questions about who is being addressed in various parts of the book and about the events to which the text refers. He compares the situation of the book of Isaiah with that of the book of Samuel. It is clear to him that Samuel did not write about those things that occurred after his death in the book that bears his name.[21] Thus, with regard to Isaiah also, when the text clearly refers to events after the time of Isaiah, the text is from a later hand.

Of course there are prophecies in Isaiah that refer to future events in general terms, especially the things of the Messianic age. But there are explicit references to Cyrus and to events of history later than Isaiah. There are also passages where Ibn Ezra has to differ with Moses Hakkohen about the identity of the people that the prophet addresses.[22] Rabbi Moses thought that the second part of the book of Isaiah referred to the restoration after the return to Jerusalem from Babylon. But that is not the case for Ibn Ezra; he thinks that some of the passages refer to the Jewish exiles of Ibn Ezra's own time.[23]

None of the great Christian medieval writers wrote a major commentary on Isaiah. The great favorites for commentaries among the biblical books were the Psalms, the letters of Paul and the Hexaemeron (the six days of creation in Genesis).[24] Although no renowned writer gave Isaiah an extended commentary, many lesser writers took up the challenge to explain this book or part of it.[25]

Reformers

The reformation opened a new era in biblical studies. First of all, the Bible was given a more prominent place in the life of the church and in that of the individual Christian. The slogan "sola scriptura" (by Scripture alone), besides being a doctrinal razor to cut away acquired beliefs, was used by those in the church who sought to drink from the wellsprings of a deeper spiritual life, and to offer this spiritual life to all Christians. The slogan also declares an independence from the traditions of the medieval church and from the undisciplined allegorical method that had developed in biblical interpretation.

Martin Luther (1483–1546) approached Isaiah in the same spirit that the Fathers had read the whole Bible.[26] For him, there seems to have been no question that anyone but Isaiah wrote the words recorded in his book. Thus, Luther says, "we rightly divide Isaiah into two books . . . in the following book [Isa 40–66] the prophet treats two matters: Prophecies concerning Christ the King and then concerning Cyrus, the king of Persia, and concerning the Babylonian captivity."[27]

At the mention of Cyrus, Luther says, "It is a marvelous thing that the Scriptures speak of this pagan king by name so long before his time."[28] Not only does Luther not see the possibility that the text might date from the time of Cyrus, he certainly does not guess that the prophet might cease to mention Cyrus again because he lost hope that Cyrus really would turn to the God of Israel.[29] In response to the Greek tale accusing Cyrus of greed, Luther says, "But this is like a lie, not to be believed, because here [Isa 45:1] we see that he was a godly man."[30]

By now in this review of opinions about Isaiah 40–66, one is not surprised when John Calvin (1509–1564), too, views Isaiah as speaking to people who would live more than one hundred and fifty years later.[31] "First, he addresses the Jews, who were soon after to be carried into that hard captivity in which they should have neither sacrifices nor prophets, and would have been destitute of all consolation, had not the Lord relieved their miseries by these predictions. Next, he addresses all the godly that should live afterwards, or that shall yet live, to encourage their heart, even when they shall appear to be reduced very low and to be utterly ruined."[32]

On the matter of Cyrus, Calvin says,

> As to the objection made by infidels, that those things might have been forged by the Jews after they were fulfilled, it is foolish and absurd that there is no necessity for refuting it. The Jews perused those prophecies, while they were held in captivity, in order that they might cherish in their hearts the hope of deliverance, and would have been entirely discouraged, if the Lord had not comforted them by such promises.[33]

Even today, the exegetical work of Calvin is highly esteemed. For the use of Isaiah in preaching, Brevard Childs passes over "much of traditional Protestant preaching" and adds, "I would, however, mention Calvin's sermons as an exception not to be lightly dismissed."[34] But it is no surprise that Calvin did not know of Second Isaiah.

Spinoza

In the history of critical biblical scholarship, a major name is that of Benedict (Baruch) Spinoza (1632–1677). Although his analyses of biblical texts are unusual for that time his orientation toward the Bible influenced many thinkers.[35] For Spinoza the discovery of the real author is an important element for understanding any part of the Bible. The scholarly interpreter must know "who it was, on what occasion, at what time, for whom, and in what language that he wrote."[36]

In *Tractatus Theologico-Politicus,* Spinoza deals mostly with the Pentateuch and the book of Joshua. He carefully and forcefully explains why Moses could not have been the author of the Pentateuch and gives his reasons for proposing Ezra as its author. When he speaks briefly, all too briefly, about Isaiah, his major point is simply that not all the words of Isaiah seem to have been preserved. Had the book of Isaiah been his real focus, he surely could have lined up the arguments (or hints, as he calls them) from Ibn Ezra and explained them thoroughly to show that Isaiah could not have written 40–66, for that was his style when he treated the Pentateuch.

Robert Lowth

After Robert Lowth had written his extremely influential work on Hebrew poetry, he published in 1778 a translation of Isaiah with an extended introduction and with copious notes.[37] Since he had read most of the major studies of Isaiah to his day, one looks to see what he thought about the idea that 40–66 came from a hand other than that in 1–39.

He never seems to really confront the issue. He recognizes that the nature of the poetry changes after chapter 39. He thinks this section contains some of the most sublime poetry in the Bible, but as regards content, he is satisfied to say that Isaiah uttered these prophecies of consolation late in the reign of Hezekiah.[38] He is at pains to show that other interpreters have stumbled on this part of Isaiah because they failed to see the various senses of the text.

Thus when he broaches what later scholarship calls the fourth servant song (Isa 52:13–53:12), he takes occasion to give an analysis of the content of 40–66.

> The subject of Isaiah's Prophecy, from the Fortieth Chapter inclusive, has hitherto been, in general, the De-liverance of the people of God. This includes in it three distinct parts: which, however, have a close connection with one another: that is, the deliverance of the Jews from the captivity of Babylon; the deliverance of the Gen-tiles from their miserable state of ignorance and idolatry; and the deliverance of Mankind from the captivity of sin and death.[39]
>
> Isaiah has not treated the three subjects as quite distinct and separate in a methodical and orderly man-ner, like a philosopher or a logician, but has taken them in their connective view; he has handled them as a prophet and a poet; he hath allegorised the former, and under the image of it has shadowed out the two latter; he has thrown them all together, has mixed one with an-other, has passed from this to that with rapid transitions, and has painted the whole with the strongest and boldest imagery.[40]

Lowth freely refers to Ibn Ezra, but he does not acknowledge or discuss the possibility that the mention of Cyrus comes from a time after the existence of that historical figure.[41] Lowth is less concerned, one might say, to find what the writer actually meant than to show that Lowth's own meaning is present in the text. "This view of [the three deliverances in 40–66] seems to afford the best method of resolving difficulties, in which Expositors are fre-quently engaged, being much divided between what is called the

Literal, and the Mystical sense, not very properly; for the mystical or spiritual sense is very often the most literal sense of all."[42]

Second Isaiah

The claim that Isaiah 40–66 was written by someone other than Isaiah, someone living late in the period of the exile, appeared in an influential "introduction" to the Old Testament written by J. G. Eichhorn (1780–83).[43] Because of Eichhorn's influence and persuasive powers and perhaps because of the data intrinsic to the issue itself, various scholars accepted the idea of a different author for the latter part of Isaiah, affirming that these chapters form a unity different from that of 1–39.

This idea of the separate authorship of Isaiah 40–66 became the accepted position in many circles, and it was adopted by various commentaries on Isaiah. Probably the most important commentary written from this perspective was that of Wilhelm Gesenius in 1821.[44] His numerous reasons for making the division may be reduced to two: the allusions in 40–66 to the Exile in Babylon and the difference in style as one moves into 40–66. A rather practical reflection that Gesenius makes is that if Isaiah had written 40–66, Jeremiah, a century later, would have appealed to those writings when he was on trial.

Joseph Addison Alexander

The position of Gesenius was attacked by the American scholar, Joseph Addison Alexander.[45] As a dyed-in-the-wool traditionalist,[46] he could not be convinced of any position which would challenge the Isaianic authorship of all the words of 40–66. For him, the creation of a "second Isaiah" is a matter of dwindling faith and a refusal to accept the supernatural powers of the prophets of God. The blame for this weakening of faith goes to German scholarship. Alexander assesses all previous and contemporary scholarship on the basis of whether it accepts Isaiah as sole author of the book.

Alexander summons all the reasons and considerations he

can for the position of authentic Isaianic authorship of 40–66. These include (1) the unlikelihood that a brilliant literary genius as the supposed "great unknown" would simply leave no trace of his existence in history or in the memory of his people, (2) the addition of these writings to the words of Isaiah, from which they do differ, (3) the long tradition of 40–66 being accepted as coming from Isaiah, (4) the New Testament's use of 40–66, (5) Ecclesiasticus's view of the book of Isaiah as a whole, and (6) the general authentic ring of Jerusalem and Judah of the eighth century even in these chapters.[47]

Alexander laments the large number of scholars who have been confused into this wrong thinking about the book of Isaiah, but he has an explanation. A weakened faith has led to the loss of belief in the predictive quality of prophecy, and even to the loss of belief in the inspiration of Scripture. That the critical scholars have given in to the desire for novelty in exposition and hypothesis results in nothing less than confusion and contradiction.[48] Alexander's erudition allows for near eloquence in denouncing the insensitivity, religious and literary, and sheer stupidity of the German spirit that, indeed, may infect (nay has already infected) beyond the borders of Germany.

Alexander, as can be expected, easily ridicules the reasoning that would rob an author of his own work on the basis of the isolated use of some unusual words on a given occasion. By way of comparison, he lists the distinctive phrases and images that Horace uses in *Ars Poetica* but which occur in none of his other writings, and on the basis of which one might try to declare *Ars Poetica* spurious.[49]

For Alexander, the peculiarity of Isa 40–66 is best explained in the following way.

Isaiah writing at a later period of life, and when withdrawn from active labour, with his view directed not to the present or a proximate futurity, but one more distant, and composing not a series of detached discourses, but a continuous unbroken prophecy, not only may, but must have differed from his former self as much as these two parts of the collection differ from each other. This antecedent probability is strengthened by the fact that similar causes have produced a still greater difference in some of the most celebrated writers, ancient and modern, who exhibit vastly more unlikeness to themselves in different parts of their acknowledged writings than the most microscopic criticism has been able to detect between the tone and manner of Isaiah's Earlier and Later Prophecies.[50]

Bernhard Duhm

Little did Alexander know that the most profound challenge to the unity of the book of Isaiah was yet to come. Bernhard Duhm's commentary on Isaiah in 1892 was to change the shape of Isaiah study perhaps for as long a time as the unity of Isaiah was never challenged.[51] Duhm not only accepted the division between and separate authorship of 1–39 and 40–66; he also added the separation of 56–66 from 40–55 and established the existence and boundaries of the four songs of the Servant of the Lord (42:1–4, 49:1–6, 50:4–9, and 52:13–53:12).

Duhm had no hesitation in denying many passages in 1–39 to the eighth century prophet. He saw a long development of the book from the time of the prophet himself into the time of the Maccabees. Probably the most striking—and least accepted—part of this very influential commentary is Duhm's idea that Second Isaiah may have lived in northern Phoenicia. This peculiarity does not diminish Duhm's certainty that 40–55 is the work of someone completely different from the eighth-century Isaiah of Jerusalem.

The position that at least 40–55 is exilic became the majority view in critical scholarship. The bases for this separation might be summarized here from a book that breathes the spirit of Duhm's age, even though at the time of this book, S. R. Driver had not yet read Duhm's commentary on Isaiah.[52] Driver has three kinds of reasons for seeing a division.

(1) Internal evidence: the audience whom the prophet addresses. Isaiah had preached to the people of Jerusalem in the

time of Ahaz and Hezekiah. He spoke to them of their current situation when he had to point out the people's failings. Here in 40–66 the words are filled with consolation and encouragement. Isaiah spoke of a judgment to come. Here the exile is in effect. Isaiah wanted to bring the unfaithful back to God. Here it is not a matter of turning people completely around but of helping them keep hope and giving them conviction that God would save them immediately.

(2) Literary style: different words and ideas. Driver lists words like "to choose" Israel as his people, "praise," "to shoot or spring forth," "to break out into singing," "pleasure," "good will" of God, and many more which occur repeatedly in 40–66 (sometimes also in 13–14 and 34–35) but not in the main sayings of Isaiah. Another list gives nine frequently occurring, forceful words in 40–66, which appear only once or twice in 1–39, and then without any special significance. In 40–66, personifications abound, especially of nature and of the city. These are rare in 1–39. One can add that the promises to the city in 1–39 concern protection and deliverance, while in 40–66 they are of return and residence.

(3) Theology: majesty versus uniqueness. God is presented in far more sweeping and universal categories in the latter part. Isa 1–39 is preoccupied with Assyria, while 40–66 constantly takes up the whole world. The remnant theme of 1–39 does not appear in 40–66. Equally, the king, whether present or future, of the first part disappears in the second section. The covenant becomes a more central expression in the second part. The purification that was to occur in the earlier part has already occurred in the remainder.

The Isaiah of Jerusalem who sometimes appears doom-filled but sometimes offers words of security and protection disappears after chapter 39. Gone is the Isaiah who sought to purify the people of the covenant, to bring them back to the God they seemed to have abandoned.

The unique blend of doom and promise, of covenant, repentance, and purification is replaced in 40–66 with a unique mixture of consolation and encouragement, of the newness of a fresh beginning in a revived life. Return and mission have taken the place of the call to follow the God who will protect the ones who remain true.

Roman Catholic Scholarship

This clear distinction appealed to most scholars who had the freedom to accept it openly. Many individual Christians and various churches feared this claim because it seemed to contradict tradition and even to oppose the New Testament. The Roman Catholic church took open action which had a decisive impact on its faithful throughout the world.

In 1893, Pope Leo XIII wrote the encyclical *Providentissimus Deus* on the study of scripture.[53] This letter required that students have solid grounding in biblical studies, and the pope encouraged biblical scholars to attempt solutions to the difficulties of the biblical texts while the scholars themselves remain docile to the teaching and decisions of the Church. To clarify this latter, Leo XIII established the Pontifical Biblical Commission to apply the official teaching in this important matter and to respond to queries sent to it.[54] In 1908, questions were sent to the Commission whether a Catholic would be permitted to accept the existence of two or more authors in the book of Isaiah for the various reasons that were being discussed. The Commission responded in the negative.

Although the decree was never taken off the books, it was virtually voided by the encyclical of Pius XII, *Divino Afflante Spiritu* in 1943.[55] He encouraged Catholic biblical scholars to study scripture with an awareness of its historical setting. The original author of a particular part of scripture lived in a specific historical period and wrote in the language of that time. Given this freedom, many Roman Catholic scholars then explained how God had spoken not only through Isaiah of Jerusalem but also through "Isaiah" of Babylon. Eventually even the decisions of the Biblical Commission were described as pastoral and limited to the time in which they were published, with the result that now Catholic scholars have "perfect freedom" with regard to those decisions of the Commission on authorship.[56]

Isaiah and the Computer

The last item for review here is clearly representative of the twentieth century, indeed, the latter part of this century. The proponents of the Second Isaiah always include in their argument linguistic data by which they claim that there is a different author in 40–66. These data were often claimed to be far too subjective, especially since most frequently only one or two tests were done on representative selections from both parts of the book of Isaiah.

The invention and development of the computer has made previously unmanageable computation now rather casual. The argument against Second Isaiah often points out that literary styles of authors differ at the writer's choice, and "Second Isaiah" is simply a different style of "First" Isaiah. But certain features of an author's style are so much a part of that person that even conscious effort on the part of the author cannot eradicate that style. This kind of literary analysis had been done on the *Federalist* papers. That study succeeded in giving the precise degree of stylistic proximity of each letter to the known styles of Hamilton and of Madison, using various criteria for the judgment.[57]

An Israeli scholar of conservative orientation set out to show by this kind of analysis that the book of Isaiah had but one author. He used forty-one different proven tests to distinguish authorship in order to see whether his claim of Isaianic unity for the whole book could be proven by this method. The statistical analysis showed that there did exist more than one author. These are the first two of his conclusions:

(a) The book is composed of two different parts, i.e. chaps. 1–35 and chaps. 40–66. (b) The most dissimilar parts are chaps. 1–12 and chaps. 40–48. Since Isaiah ben Amoz was beyond any doubt the author of the first, he cannot have written the latter.[58]

Not all scholars will agree with the claim that Isaiah wrote every word in 1–12, but Radday's own change of opinion itself is noteworthy.

Reading Isaiah

To conclude this review, one must say that Isaiah has not always been a transparent book for everyone. Previous ways of reading the book continue to influence the modern reader. It is hard for some not to read a particular verse of Isaiah without hearing the whole of Isaiah. But one's attention cannot take in all of Isaiah at once. And even if one could do that feat, interest and attraction would sift out and arrange what the reader wanted to hear or what the reader claimed to hear. So too with the trained scholar. These differences of attention and emphasis lead to differences among the interpreters of Isaiah. Yet the quest for the real Isaiah continues to attract many scholars.

Notes

1. For a general survey of the Dead Sea Scrolls, see Geza Vermes, *The Dead Sea Scrolls: Qumran in Perspective* (London: Collins, 1977).

2. For a further description of the Isaiah scroll, see Gaalyah Cornfeld, *Archaeology of the Bible: Book by Book* (New York: Harper & Row, 1976) 157.

3. In place of this commentary, there survive only some homilies of Origen on Isaiah.

4. Often when Jerome cites the Jewish tradition, or even refers to Jewish scholars he had learned from, he is simply relying on the Jews whom Origen had consulted and whose positions he records. See Seraphinus Gozzo, "De S. Hieronymi commentario in Isaiae librum," *Antonianum* 35 (1960) 49–80, 169–214; on this point, 60–61 with the notes there.

5. Of the many studies on Origen, one might mention those of Daniélou and de Lubac.

6. Greek text only, *Der Jesajakommentar* (ed. Joseph Ziegler, Die Griechischen Christlichen Schriftsteller; Berlin: Academie, 1975).

7. See, e.g., Timothy D. Barnes, *Constantine and Eusebius* (Cambridge: Harvard University, 1981) 102–4.

8. Latin text only in *S. Hieronymi Presbyteri Opera, Partes*

1,2 and *1,2A* (Corpus Christianorum, Series Latina; Turnholt: Brepols, 1963).

9. Besides the article of Gozzo in n. 4 above, see F.-M. Abel, "Le commentaire de Saint Jérome sur Isaïe," *Revue Biblique* 25, ns 13 (1916) 200–225.

10. C.C.S.L. 73:454–55.

11. C.C.S.L. 73A:504.

12. See Gozzo, art. cit., pp. 57–63.

13. The commentary may well be spurious. It is not in Migne, nor even mentioned in the article on Ephrem in the *NCE*. It is not used in Xavier Ducros, "Le dogme de l'Inspiration chez saint Ephrem d'apres ses commentaires de l'Ancient Testament," *Mélanges F. Cavallera* (Toulouse: Institut Catholique, 1948) 163–77.

14. The authentic commentary ends with Isa 8:10. A recent edition and translation is Jean Chrysostome, *Commentaire sur Isaïe* (ed. Jean Dumortier, Sources Chrétiennes; Paris: du Cerf, 1983).

15. In PG 70. See also Alexander Kerrigan, *St. Cyril of Alexandria: Interpreter of the Old Testament* (AnBib; Rome: Biblical Institute, 1952).

16. Recent edition, Théodoret de Cyr, *Commentaire sur Isaïe* (ed. Jean-Noel Guinot, 3 vols; Sources Chrétiennes; Paris: du Cerf, 1980, 1982, 1984).

17. See the text of the "Martyrdom and Ascension of Isaiah" in James Charlesworth, ed., *The Old Testament Pseudepigrapha* (Garden City: Doubleday, 1985) 2:143–76.

18. They say he later reduced the six to two: justice and charity. See Mishnah, tractate Makshirin 24a, cited in *The Jewish Encyclopedia* (1901) 6:636.

19. Baba bathra 14b.

20. Bernard M. Casper, *An Introduction to Jewish Bible Commentary* (New York: Thomas Yoseloff, 1960) 70.

21. Abraham ben Meir Ibn Ezra, *The Commentary of Ibn Ezra on Isaiah* (ed. M. Friedlander; London, 1873; repr. New York: Philipp Feldheim, 1948) 170. See also U. Simon, "Ibn Ezra between Medievalism and Modernism: the Case of Isaiah xl–lxvi," *SVT* 36 [Salamanca Volume, 1983] (1985).

22. R. K. Harrison, *Introduction to the Old Testament* (Grand Rapids: Eerdmans, 1969), 763, 765, suggests that Moses ben Samuel Ibn Gekatilla (whom Ibn Ezra calls Moses Hakkohen) inspired Ibn Ezra to question Isaiah's authorship of the whole book. Given Ibn Ezra's otherwise independent thought, this supposition of dependence is probably not accurate.

23. *The Commentary of Ibn Ezra,* 236.

24. Beryl Smalley, "The Bible in the Medieval Schools," in *The Cambridge History of the Bible, Volume 2: The West from the Fathers to the Reformation* (Cambridge: The University, 1969) 205.

25. See the *Repertorium Biblicum Medii Aevi* (Madrid, 1950–) by F. Stegmüller for authors and manuscripts. See also the list in Luis Alonso-Schökel, "Isaie," *DS* 7 (1971) 2078. Mention should be made of Andrew of St. Victor, "In Isaiam," which exists only in manuscript, and of Thomas of Aquin, "In Isaiam," which can be found in volumes 18 and 19 of *Omnia Opera* (Vives edition; Paris, 1882). There is a copy of Thomas' comments on Isa 34:1–50:1 in his own handwriting. (Information from Dr. Wanda Cizewski.)

26. Martin Luther, *Lectures on Isaiah, Chapters 40–66* (Luther's Works; Saint Louis: Concordia, 1972).

27. Ibid., 3.

28. Ibid., 121.

29. Such has been the solution of various scholars; recently Carroll Stuhlmueller, "Deutero-Isaiah (chaps. 40–55): Major Transitions in the Prophet's Theology and in Contemporary Scholarship," *CBQ* 42 (1980) 1–29.

30. Op. cit., 122.

31. John Calvin, *Commentary on the Book of the Prophet Isaiah* (5 vols.; Grand Rapids: Eerdmans, n.d.).

32. Ibid., 3:197.

33. Ibid., 3:390.

34. Brevard S. Childs, *Old Testament Books for Pastor and Teacher* (Philadelphia: Westminster, 1977), 74.

35. Most of his thought on biblical interpretation is found in Benedict de Spinoza, *Tractatus Theologico-Politicus* (London: Trubner, 1862).

36. Ibid., 148.

37. Robert Lowth, *Isaiah: A New Translation with a Preliminary Dissertation and Notes* (London: Nichols, 1778). His work on poetry was published in Latin, *De Sacra Poesi Hebraeorum Praelectiones,* 1753.

38. Ibid., 183 of the notes.

39. Ibid., 236.

40. Ibid., 237.

41. He does mention that some scholars ("it is by many learned interpreters supposed") refer chapter 63 to Judas Maccabeus (second century BCE) and his victories. But Lowth does not consider that the text might date from after the historical person referred to. He simply says that nothing that Judas or the Hasmoneans accomplished deserves "the Prophet's lofty prediction." Moreover, "the Idumea of the Prophet's time was quite simply a different country from that which Judas conquered," ibid., 265–66.

42. Ibid., 237.

43. J. G. Eichhorn, *Einleitung in das Alte Testament* (3 vols., 1780–1783).

44. Wilhelm Gesenius, *Philologisch-kritischer und historischer Commentar über den Jesaia* (3 vols; Leipzig, 1821).

45. Joseph Addison Alexander, *The Prophecies of Isaiah* (2 vols. new ed.); New York: Charles Scribners, 1865.

46. Alexander was the son of Archibald Alexander, founder of Princeton Theological Seminary.

47. Ibid., 1:66–67.

48. Alexander, ibid., 1:16, lists scores of opinions which radically differ from and conflict with each other.

49. Ibid., 1:19.

50. Ibid., 1:65–66.

51. Bernhard Duhm, *Das Buch Jesaja* (5th ed, Göttingen: Vandenhoeck & Ruprecht, 1968). Edward J. Young devotes to Duhm the largest segment of his review, "The Study of Isaiah Since the Time of Joseph Addison Alexander," in *Studies in Isaiah* (Grand Rapids: Eerdmans, 1954) 9–101.

52. S. R. Driver, *An Introduction to the Old Testament* (2d ed, Meridian repr.; New York: World, 1965), 205–46 on Isaiah.

53. Translation in *Rome and the Study of Scripture* (5th ed; St. Meinrad, Indiana: Grail, 1953) 1–29.

54. Translation with quite dated comments in *A Catholic Commentary on Holy Scripture* (ed. Bernard Orchard, et al.; New York: Thomas Nelson and Sons, 1953) 67–75.

55. *Rome and the Study of Scripture,* 79–107.

56. See Raymond Brown, "Catechetics in an Age of Theological Change," *Origins* 2 (1973) 677, 679–80, 689–92: on the Commission decisions, 680.

57. Ivor S. Francis, "An Exposition of a Statistical Approach to the Federalist Dispute," in *The Computer and Literary Style* (ed. Jacob Leed; Kent, Ohio: Kent State University, 1966) 38–78.

58. Yehuda T. Radday, *The Unity of Isaiah in the Light of Statistical Linguistics* (Publications de l'Institut de Recherche et d'Histoire des Textes; Hildesheim: H. A. Gerstenberg, 1973).

4.

Isaiah and Language

"The style is the man himself." This saying rings true not just for individuals and their personalities but especially for a person's use of language. Every human being reveals something of the self in the selection of words used to convey ideas. Both the words one uses and especially the ways in which they are put together tell much about one's self, one's self-perception, and the perception of other persons and things.

Words are the expression of thought. But thought is so intimately connected with the words of a language that some psychologists have insisted that the two are inseparably bound together.[1] A child does not think human thoughts without knowing the words which embody them. In order to think, children must learn the words with which to think. And the words people use reveal much.

In the Old Testament, the way a prophet responds to the call of God can indicate for the reader some of the differences among prophets. Jeremiah's response to the Lord who appoints him "a prophet to the nations" is the cry "Ah, ah, ah, Lord God, behold, I cannot speak, for I am a child" (Jer 1:6).[2] Isaiah's response, on the other hand, to the presence of God employs true words from the start, and these words are poetic.

> I am a man of unclean lips, and I dwell in the midst of a
> people of unclean lips; for my eyes have seen the King,
> the Lord of hosts.
>
> Isa 6:5

37

Isaiah is a man of words, stunning and beautiful words, words which reveal his inmost thoughts and experiences. His words make up some of the most powerful and memorable speeches in human history.

Testimonies of the loftiness of Isaiah's language are not difficult to find. One quotation from Matthew Arnold can suffice:

> I keep asking myself about Isaiah. Taking him merely as poetry and literature,—which is not, I will readily add, to take him in his entirety,—I consider the question very important. I rate the value of the operation of poetry and literature upon men's minds extremely high: and from no poetry and literature, not even from our own Shakespeare and Milton, great as they are and our own as they are, have I, for my part, received so much delight and stimulus as from Homer and Isaiah.[3]

Concreteness

Perhaps the most striking features of Isaiah's speeches are the drama and concreteness of his language. His collected oracles begin, not with some universal ideas of goodness or beauty, but with the cry to the heavens and to the earth that they might hear the case and complaint that he has to make:

> Hear, O heavens, and give ear, O earth;
>   for the Lord has spoken.
>
> 1:2a

This speech is language of concrete images. The ideas continue to manifest a preference for real objects[4] in the reference to a personal relation of parent and child:

> Sons have I reared and brought up,
>   but they have rebelled against me
>
> 1:2b

rather than an abstract Creator-creature relationship. Then follow the ox and the ass and their owners, the crib and its concreteness:

> The ox knows its owner,
>   and the ass its master's crib;
> but Israel does not know,
>   my people does not understand.

1:3

Isaiah declares that the city will be punished by desolation, but instead of enumerating the actual ruins he depicts the city as a forlorn woman and as a lean-to abandoned in a field (1:8, 21). Isaiah speaks with concreteness in order to communicate the message that he has received.

The prophets, aware of being the recipients of a very important and significant message, sought to find the most compelling language to convey the message. The prophets endeavored to make the delivery of their message more forceful by the use of comparisons. The similes and metaphors of Isaiah present dramatic and powerful images which allow the hearers and later readers to experience fully the dynamism of the prophetic word. J. Cheryl Exum has shown the sharpness and variety in Isaiah's use of metaphor in three passages.[5]

Comparisons

Isa 30:12–14 compares the people's rejection of God's word to the cracking of a high wall that has begun to bulge (v 13). Rather than be content with a statement of that idea and a description of a cracking wall, the prophet was so taken up with this comparison of rejection to a crack that the breaking wall itself is compared to a shattering vessel (v 14). One simile leads into and forms the basis of the other. The poet-prophet has taken care to select words in the first simile that convey the idea of total collapse, while the second simile emphasizes that the shattering will be entire and complete. In other words, the prophet chose words that had dramatic power and startling vividness in order to convey forcefully the dire warning he was to give on that particular occasion.

A second use of simile employs two comparisons, a lion who defends his prey and birds who flutter to deliver (31:4–5). These two images are used in immediate proximity so that they can clarify and reinforce each other. The picture of a lion over its prey is rather ambiguous without the undeniably protective image of the birds. Here, too, the choice of concrete comparisons drives home the intent and meaning of the prophet's message, a complex and qualified one.

Exum, thirdly, studies Isa 29:1–14, also for its metaphors and similes. The passage contains two poems, which when set next to each other not only form a contrast but also give a combined meaning. Isa 29:1–8 depicts Ariel (Zion) besieged and humiliated by a "multitude of foreigners," who themselves are humiliated by God in his deliverance of Zion. The prophet says that the attackers will be deceived just as is one who dreams of having the physical needs of hunger and thirst fulfilled—but it is only a dream.

The second poem, Isa 29:9–14, forms a unit[6] which questions the promised salvation of vv 6–8. The deed that Yahweh might perform now becomes incomprehensible. Those who should be able to see cannot any more, and even the learned are suddenly incapable of the simple task of reading a book. The ambiguity and precariousness of the situation strikes the reader today as much as it did the people who heard Isaiah himself speak these words.

The two poems form a complex literary structure with interrelated ideas and reappearing literary devices. The first tie is simply the free and forceful use of similes of vision. The two poems are further linked by two references to cultic activity. The opening reference is to repeated acts of worship

> Add year to year;
>   let the feasts run their round.
>
>   29:1

and the closing reference castigates inauthentic religious ritual

> Because this people draw near with their mouth
> and honor me with their lips,
> while their hearts are far from me . . .
>
> 29:13

Finally, the dream of deliverance is balanced by the choice to remain in the darkness of incomprehension.

Exum's study shows how intense is the focus of the prophet's vision and how carefully the prophet selects the language of simile to convey the intensity of that vision.

Creativity within Traditional Forms

While the forcefulness of Isaiah's similes reveals his creativity, other clear examples of Isaiah's originality are the changes he made in traditional prophetic speech forms. The standard way a prophet of doom announced judgment was to give a reason for the judgment (often an accusation of wrong doing by individuals or by the people as a whole) and then to declare the punishment which was to come. The two sections form the usual elements of a double verbal structure. "Because you have done such-and-such, therefore such-and-such will happen to you." Or in the words of Isaiah:

> Because this people have refused the waters of Shiloah
> that flow gently, and melt in fear before Rezin and the
> son of Remaliah; therefore, behold, the Lord is bringing
> up against them the waters of the River, mighty and
> many, the king of Assyria and all his glory.
>
> Isa 8:6–7

Roy Melugin studies three sayings where Isaiah makes significant modifications in that form.[7]

In Isa 30:15–17, the traditional pattern of this prophetic form is broken first by beginning an oracle of doom (judgment) with a word of promise (salvation),

In returning and rest you shall be saved;
in quietness and in trust shall be your strength.

Isa 30:15

Then an accusation follows, "You were not willing; you said 'No! On horses we will flee.' " Isaiah builds an accusation out of a quotation about the people's unwillingness to receive the word (of promise) from God only here. This announcement of judgment strikingly and creatively takes up and turns around a promise that had previously been given.

A second example of how Isaiah used the traditional prophetic form (accusation and announcement) in his own way occurs in Isa 28:7–13. Isaiah here modifies the usual form to express his theological view that the people's refusal to obey God later causes their inability to respond to God. The specific modification includes the introduction of what critics call disputation, in which opponents question some of the possibilities the speaker mentions. This disputation, 28:9–10, serves as the means of connecting the accusation and announcement, which elsewhere are often joined simply by a "therefore." Isaiah has again put his distinctive mark on a traditional form.

The third passage Melugin studies, 28:14–22, contains the famous statement,

Behold, I am laying in Zion for a foundation
a stone, a tested stone,
a precious cornerstone, of a sure foundation:
"He who believes will not be in haste."

28:16

The peculiarity here is that this word of promise is inserted into the middle of the form, falling between accusation of wrong-doing (distrust) and announcement of disaster. Often a critic will say that a promise in the midst of a judgment speech must be a later insertion. Melugin, however, argues that here Isaiah himself has included this reference to God's promise in the midst of judgment to show not only God's willingness to save but also to show that God offered *conditional* salvation. Indeed, the sting of judgment would be all the sharper if during that judgment the accused remembered that punishment really had not been inevitable. Thus, Isaiah modified traditional structures of prophetic speech to convey his distinctive insights and message.

Isaiah could and did make changes in the established prophetic form of the judgment speech. This very claim reflects the generally accepted idea that in the literature of ancient Israel, as in ancient Near Eastern literature generally, there were clearly established inherited forms of expression and communication. The prophetic speech forms are one category of literary forms that the prophets were expected to use.[8]

Parallel Pairs

A different major approach to the literary study of the Hebrew poetry focuses more narrowly on words. Anyone who attempted to speak in poetic form in ancient Israel was bound by the special, well-known, and required use of certain words. Poetry among the ancient Semites was constituted by the device of parallelism, the essential aspect of which is that one line is picked up by the next line either by repetition or by modification. This procedure naturally requires a poet to have in memory enough similar or related words, so that one need not repeat the same word in both halves of the parallelism.

One of the most fascinating discoveries during the past fifty years of Old Testament studies is that the Israelite poets used the poetic verbal structures that appear in the Ugaritic texts of the second millennium BCE. Many generations before Israel had the land, poets of Canaan developed literary conventions about which words worked together. The story of how this discovery gradually developed is indeed fascinating.[9] The reality is even more striking: the Israelite prophets often used selected words in the same order as did the poets who worshiped the gods of Canaan several centuries before the prophets of Israel.

Some examples of this phenomenon may be helpful to see how it actually functions. Isa 1:2 begins, "Hear, O heavens, and give ear, O earth." The verbs "hear" and "give ear" (Hebrew *šmʿ*

and *h'zyn*) form a parallel pair. The pair appears in Ugaritic as "hear" (*šmʿ*) and "ear" (*udn*), and occurs twice in situations where a person tries to get someone else's attention. One should note that Ugaritic *udn* is phonetically equivalent to the Hebrew *'zn* ("ear") and *h'zyn* ("to give ear"). The nouns "heaven" and "earth" (Hebrew *šmym* and *'rṣ*), two words which form a frequent pair in the Bible, occur twice in parallel in Ugarit (*šmm* and *arṣ*).[10]

The next verse, 1:3, contains the complaint, "Israel does not know (*ydʿ*), my people does not understand (*bn*)." This pair occurs in similar parallel construction and in exact equivalents in Ugaritic at least three times. The pair "enemy" (*'wyb*) and "foe" (*ṣr*) in Isa 1:24 appears in Ugaritic in the phonetically equivalent *ib* parallel with *ṣrt*.

Isaiah, like all other Israelite prophets, inherited a poetic tradition which he learned and used well. The prophet was not simply given words directly by God. He was charged with the task of preaching the word of God, but he also learned how to preach in a poetic style that went back centuries before his time—before the time that Israel lived in the land of Canaan.

Words and Insight

Isaiah, a master of words, also experienced God in an extraordinary way. He spoke the word of God in well chosen words and with the urgency of one overwhelmed with the presence of God.[11] R. B. Y. Scott has proposed that this prophet's inspiration was often tied to specific words, that his initial insight or revelation was connected to the sound of the Hebrew words which conveyed the idea.[12] Isaiah was struck by the similar yet different sounds of words which depicted the condition that the prophet saw or the event that the prophet knew would be inevitable.

The most frequently cited example of this is the closing of the song of the vineyard, Isa 5:1–7.

And he looked for justice,
but behold, bloodshed;

> for righteousness,
>> but behold, a cry!

Isa 5:7

Isaiah says that God had looked for justice (*mišpat*) but he finds bloodshed (*mišpah*) and instead of righteousness (*ṣedaqah*) there is only a cry (*ṣeʿaqah*) (v 7). Scott proposes that the prophet had received his initial revelation in private as he reflected on the actions of the leaders of the people and on the treatment of the poor and powerless in his own society. The prophet later on elaborated this private oracle and worked it up into the parable of chapter 5. Now the original saying serves simply as the climax of the parable.

Isa 30:15 also represents a good example of assonance, here inverted, *bešubah wanaḥat tiwwašeʿûn*, ("in turning and rest you shall be saved," 30:15a). Other examples that Scott finds are 1:16, 23; 3:1; 8:6; 9:17; 29:2; 30:1; 31:1, 2. The divine inspiration to Isaiah seems to have been occasionally conditioned by words and the sounds that they made.

Pure Poetry

There remains a final proposal regarding the literary accomplishment and poetic nature of the Isaiah collection. It is noteworthy that the book of Isaiah is mostly poetry, while the book of Jeremiah clearly comprises sections of prose and poetry that rather sharply contrast with each other. A. Graeme Auld[13] further points out that the poetry in Isaiah does not always appear to function in the service of an inseparable religious message. There seems to be a special delight in literary beauty itself.[14]

Auld recalls that Hermann Gunkel's analysis of the legends in Genesis concluded that these legends of Israel's early ancestors began and flourished as folk-stories and only later were "spiritualized." What began as entertainment later carried a religious meaning. Auld wonders whether one should suggest that the Isaiah collection in its first instance was a collection of poetry which later was "accommodated to prophecy." In other words, the figure of Isaiah took on more the characteristics of a prophet as his words were reinterpreted in situations that were increasingly more religious and less directed toward literary achievement as such.

This proposal is unusual, but, as Auld points out, it is no more shocking or revolutionary than Gunkel's analysis of the legends in Genesis. Only time will tell what decision the majority of scholars will give regarding this proposal. The very proposal itself points out the ambiguity and great wealth of ideas in the Isaiah material, with the result that Isaiah can legitimately be seen in the variety of ways that the later chapters of this book will show. In the meantime, one might rest content with the assessment of Isaiah's language and message from a German scholar who has published probably the most respected commentary on a different prophet.[15]

> Isaiah is the prophet who as none other before or after him had the office of proclaiming the majesty, freedom and mystery of 'the Holy One of Israel,' not abstractly but with an increasing sense of awe and a directness of address within the historical situation of his time. Isaiah's language is, with all its brilliance and power of words, a deft instrument for the message about the grandeur and freedom of his Lord in his historical coming to his people and to the world of the peoples.[16]

Notes

1. See, for example, L. S. Vygotsky, *Thought and Language* (Cambridge: M.I.T., 1962).

2. This reading is from the Douay-Rheims translation, the seventeenth century English rendering of Jerome's Latin. Jerome's *a a a* translates well the Hebrew *'ahah* in this context.

3. Matthew Arnold, *Isaiah of Jerusalem: in the Authorized English Version with an Introduction, Corrections, and Notes* (London: Macmillan, 1883) 4.

4. Wildberger speaks of the *Anschaulichkeit* ("vividness") of Isaiah's diction. Hans Wildberger, *Jesaja* (3 vols., BK; Neukirchen-Vluyn: Neukirchener, 1965–82) 1694.

5. J. Cheryl Exum, "Of Broken Pots, Fluttering Birds, and Visions in the Night," *CBQ* 43 (1981) 331–52.

6. Exum here goes against many commentators who see in vv 9–14 three small sections of two verses each, e.g., G. Fohrer, *Das Buch Jesajas* (3 vols., Zürcher Bibelkommentare; Zürich: Zwingli, 1960–64) 2 (2d ed, 1967):76–81.

7. Roy F. Melugin, "The Conventional and the Creative in Isaiah's Judgment Oracles," *CBQ* 36 (1974) 301–11.

8. See Melugin, p. 301. For a good introduction to Form Criticism applied to the prophetic literature, see Gene Tucker, *Form Criticism of the Old Testament* (Guides to Biblical Scholarship; Philadelphia: Fortress, 1971) 54–77, and in greater detail, John H. Hayes, ed., *Old Testament Form Criticism* (San Antonio: Trinity University, 1974).

9. For a review of the development of this research, see William R. Watters, *Formula Criticism and the Poetry of the Old Testament* (BZAW 138; Berlin: de Gruyter, 1976) 20–27. The remarks there about the scholar who first identified the phenomenon of parallel pairs can be corrected by Mitchell Dahood, "Ugaritic-Hebrew Parallel Pairs," in *Ras Shamra Parallels* (ed. Loren Fisher, AO 49; Rome: Biblical Institute, 1972), for the discoverer was C. Virolleaud in 1933, not H. L. Ginsberg in 1934.

10. The frequency of the pair in the Bible and the infrequency of it in Ugaritic is not surprising, because only a few works of Ugaritic literature still exist and are accessible. What survives does so mainly by chance, since the city and its culture disappeared in 1400 BCE.

11. This is emphasized by the title of H. Rencken's book on Isaiah 1–12, *Isaiah, the Prophet of the Presence of God.*

12. R. Y. B. Scott, "The Literary Structure of Isaiah's Oracles," in *Studies in Old Testament Prophecy* (FS Theodore H. Robinson; Edinburgh: T. & T. Clark, n. d., repr. 1957) 175–86.

13. A. Graeme Auld, "Poetry, Prophecy, Hermeneutic: Recent Studies in Isaiah," *SJT* 32 (1980) 567–81.

14. An extended study of the aural and visual beauty in Isaiah 1–35 is found in Luis Alonso-Schökel, *Estudios de Poética Hebrea* (Barcelona: Juan Flors, 1963) 359–534.

15. Walther Zimmerli, *Ezekiel* (2 vols., Hermeneia; Philadelphia: Fortress, 1879–83).

16. Walther Zimmerli, "Verküngdigung und Sprache der
Botschaft Jesajas," in *Fides et Cummunicatio* (FS Martin Doerne;
Göttingen: Vandenhoeck & Ruprecht, 1970) 441–54.

5.

Isaiah and Wisdom

Prophets have often been contrasted by scholars to those who played other social roles in ancient Israel, but such contrasts appear even in some biblical statements. Jer 18:18 speaks of three categories:

> For the law shall not perish from the priest,
>   nor counsel from the wise,
>   nor the word from the prophet.

The distinctions are clear. From a different perspective, however, one might justly compare prophet and wise man in addition to contrasting them as Jeremiah does.

What is the historical origin of the office of the prophet? Some scholarly approaches have found the origin of prophetic activity parallel to that of the priesthood. In such a view, prophets would have some of the features and functions of the early priests.[1] Now, it is true that Jeremiah and Ezekiel were of priestly families,[2] and that Ezekiel surely had performed priestly duties.[3] But it is not at all clear that Isaiah had any priestly ancestry or background. The suggestion for Isaiah is that he shares to some degree the orientation of the second group in the verse from Jeremiah. Isaiah, for some, is connected with the wisdom tradition of Israel.

The prophet Amos might stem from a wisdom background, according to some interpreters.[4] Amos has only few hints of priestly connections, but he does seem to exhibit some obvious traits of the "clan wisdom" that flourished among the tribes of Israel. Some scholars perceive a rural quality of Amos's imagery which witnesses to the village or small-community setting for his experience and orientation.

Wisdom and Jerusalem

But Isaiah is a different case. Amos was from the country; Isaiah, from the city. Amos moved from one kingdom to another; Isaiah seems to have remained only in Jerusalem.[5] The very first chapter of Isaiah has Zion in prominence:

> The daughter of Zion is left . . .
>   like a besieged city.
>
> 1:8

> How·the faithful city
>   has become a harlot,
>   she that was full of justice!
>
> 1:21

> Afterward you shall be called
>   the city of righteousness,
>   the faithful city.
>
> 1:26

> Zion shall be redeemed by justice,
>   and those in her who repent, by righteousness.
>
> 1:27

If Isaiah came from a wisdom background, that wisdom would have been of a more urban nature, more court-oriented. And this is precisely what the data show. Critics have found in the narratives about Isaiah the picture of a man who is well qualified to move in elite circles and to have easy access to the king.[6]

A study of Robert T. Anderson proposes an attractive alternative to the idea that Isaiah had a priestly background.[7] Anderson suggests that Isaiah had been an employee of the royal court as a scribe. Although Anderson does not discuss wisdom, the work of the scribe in the eighth century would have included the education of the children of the royal family and of the nobility in general. There could well have been formal schools in ancient Israel, especially in Jerusalem.[8] Anderson suggests that Isaiah may at one time, during much of Ahaz's reign, have left the royal employ, but returned to it with the accession of Hezekiah.[9]

Wisdom Words

J. Fichtner, earlier, had studied the language of Isaiah to see what wisdom connections there may be between Isaiah's words and the sayings of the wise men of ancient Israel.[10] Isa 1:3,

> The ox knows its owner,
>   and the ass its master's crib;
> but Israel does not know,
>   my people does not understand,

is a parable-like comparison for Yahweh's people who do not serve their Lord. Such a parable seems to come from the wisdom setting where interest in different animal species is paired with the use of animals in descriptions of human behavior.

Perhaps Isa 3:10–11 is the clearest passage of a fully traditional wisdom saying in Isaiah.

> Tell the righteous that it shall be well with them,
>   for they shall eat the fruit of their deeds.
> Woe to the wicked! It shall be ill with him,
>   for what his hands have done shall be done to him.

It declares that the lot of the righteous and that of the wicked are the direct results of their own doings. Thus, the saying further sets the two groups as the two contradictory and mutually exclusive possibilities for human existence. This manner of teaching by parable, so characteristic of wisdom, is further represented by both the parable of the vineyard in 5:1–7 and the parable of the farmer in 28:24–29.

The collected sayings of Isaiah of Jerusalem also contain some resistance to and critique of wisdom and its proponents. The woe-saying at 5:21,

> Woe to those who are wise in their own eyes,
>   and shrewd in their own sight!

warns certain of the wise men of the dangers of their profession. The withdrawal of wisdom from the wise is one of the threats Isaiah makes in 29:14,

> The wisdom of their wise men shall perish,
>   and the discernment of their discerning men shall be
>   hid.

Fichtner's conclusion is that although Isaiah had been among the wise, he left that group to become a prophet. This change of position and accompanying change of perspective explains the criticism he later had of some of the wise. Isaiah even warns the wise of Egypt in 19:11–13. Their condition too is a reversal and the opposite of what one expects for wise men.

Wise Man vs. Prophet?

This prophetic critique of the wise has also served as the basis on which some scholars have denied the prophet's connection with the wisdom movement. Johannes Lindblom points to the tension between prophet and wise man.[11] The prophets were well aware of the wisdom for which some foreign peoples were renowned,[12] and the prophets knew that the "wise men" formed a particular group within Israel.[13]

But when the Israelite wise men preferred their insights over against the word of God which comes through the prophet, then the prophets could condemn and heap scorn on the wise and underline the futility of reliance on the human rather than on the divine vision and power which comes through the prophet.

Woe to those who are wise in their own eyes,
    and shrewd in their own sight!

Isa 5:21

Although prophets sometimes use the language of wisdom, and certainly use some of their ideas, often the language of wisdom is turned against the professional wise men.

William McKane also stresses the separation of prophet from wise man.[14] He especially argues that the old wisdom of the wise was more an insight into practical situations and was geared to political advantage and advancement. Statesmanship was the real essence of the old wisdom and the "fear of God" was not an essential ingredient of it. McKane has to disagree with von Rad who claims that the old wisdom knew its limits and had the honesty to admit that wisdom could deal only with certain issues and could not approach the realm where God existed and carried on his hidden activity and from which he issued his inscrutable decrees.[15]

McKane claims that the old wisdom was more specifically statecraft that saw the needs of the situation not as circumscribed by some moral requirements deriving from some other order. Indeed, Isaiah attacks that older wisdom when he derides those who say

Let him make haste, let him speed his work
    that we may see it;
let the purpose of the Holy One of Israel draw near,
    and let it come, that we may know it!

Isa 5:19

The political realm depended on no other realm. Religious though they might have been, the wise courtiers of the Israelite kings offered their advice and policies on the basis of experience and reason. This understanding of the old wisdom is the basis for denying a connection between Isaiah and wisdom.

Wisdom Content and Context

A very staunch defender of the idea that Isaiah has important influences from wisdom is William J. Whedbee.[16] He studies some of the same texts that Fichtner studied but he gives them a fuller analysis. His findings support those of Fichtner and go beyond that study by showing in those sayings a large number of ideas from the wisdom tradition and many connections to works of wisdom literature. The parable of the ox and the ass and that of the vineyard are found to have deep wisdom ties.

Even greater attention is given the parable of the farmer, Isa 28:23–29.

> Give ear, and hear my voice;
>   hearken, and hear my speech.
> Does he who plows for sowing plow continually?
>   does he continually open and harrow his ground?
> When he has leveled its surface,
>   does he not scatter dill, sow cummin,
> and put in wheat in rows,
>   and barley in its proper place,
>   and spelt as the border?
> For he is instructed aright;
>   his God teaches him.

The wisdom character of the passage is rather clear, but the correct interpretation has been debated. Does the simple description of the soil and crop mean that God surely will bring an end to the threat of danger and bring salvation and security? Whedbee cannot agree that the saying should be read as an unequivocal promise. Rather, the prophet is "giving his reflections and arguments in the present crisis of faith." "Yahweh, like the wise farmer, will not continue to do the same thing." Isaiah is saying in effect, "Since we may count on God being as wise as the farmer, we may trust that he will not punish forever."[17]

Then Whedbee investigates proverbial speech in Isaiah. Isa 10:15 offers this example,

> Shall the ax vaunt itself over him who hews with it,
>   or the saw magnify itself against him who wields it?
> As if a stick should wield him who lifts it,
>   or as if a staff should lift him who is not wood!

Another complaint against the pride of the people is the proverb-like speech of Isa 29:16,

> Is the potter regarded as the clay?
> Can something made say of its maker,
>   "He did not make me"?
> Or something fashioned say of its fashioner,
>   "He has no sense"?

Such sayings reflect wisdom as practiced in Israel. The prophet uses a wisdom form to show the people where improvement in behavior and attitude is required.

In addition, a rather recently discovered wisdom literary form, the "summary-appraisal form," is found twice in the prophet Isaiah.[18] This form serves to give a reflective conclusion to whatever prophetic speech precedes it. Isa 17:14b is a good example:

> This is the portion of those who despoil us,
>   and the lot of those who plunder us.

Other important wisdom forms and elements that Whedbee finds in Isaiah are the woe-sayings and the talk of counsel and counselors.[19] Gerstenberger had proposed that the origin of the woe sayings was the wisdom tradition among the tribes of Israel.[20] In such a perspective, Isa 5:18,

> Woe to those
>   who draw iniquity with cords of falsehood,
>   who draw sin as with cart ropes,

would be calling such actions foolishness. Whedbee accepts this view and shows that not only does the form of the woe saying seem to have a wisdom origin but also the content of these sayings reveal that Isaiah was influenced by the broad stream of wisdom ethos and moral behavior advocated by the early forms of Israelite wisdom. The frequent occurrences of counsel and counselors in

Isaiah betray his activity in the court and among its groups of wisdom professionals.

Israel's unique historical experience produced in Isaiah a new development in the wisdom tradition, a kind of mixture of wisdom and history. Hans-Jürgen Hermisson points out that the God of Isaiah is not the God of traditional wisdom who stands apart from history and from the events of political life.[21]

Isaiah's God is one who, though wise, intrudes in history. Yahweh in Isaiah's eyes is the same God who fought in the holy wars of old and who reveals himself in historical events. Isaiah takes much from wisdom, but that wisdom is used to express Isaiah's distinctive idea that Yahweh has a plan in history.[22] When Isa 28:29 proclaims of Yahweh

> He is wonderful in counsel,
>   and excellent in wisdom,

the prophet is combining wisdom and history. Thus a distinctive part of the wisdom tradition is transformed by the prophet.

Tôrah as Wisdom Teaching

Soon after Whedbee's work, Joseph Jensen published his study of Isaiah, which focuses on the word *tôrah* as Isaiah used it.[23] Jensen demonstrates that, in the appearances of this word in Isaiah, *tôrah* refers to the whole teaching of the tradition, the wisdom tradition, rather than to any "prophetic torah," or to a legal torah understood as the collection of laws. The use of the word "torah" as the whole written legal tradition (the Pentateuch) appears in literature only after the time of Isaiah. That usage is found, for example, in Deuteronomy.

When Isaiah uses "torah," he is carrying on a debate with the wisdom leaders of his day, trying to show them that they have failed to live up to the demands and expectations of their own tradition. An example is Isa 1:10,

> Hear the word of the Lord,
>   you rulers of Sodom!

Give ear to the teaching [*tôrah*] of our God,
   you people of Gomorrah!

Other occurrences are 2:3; 5:24; 8:16, 20; 30:9. Isaiah turns the words of the wise men back against them because they neglected Yahweh and the wisdom that derives from him. Their own lives were lacking in fervor.

Jensen's later commentary on Isaiah[24] shows the specific passages that are richly indebted to the wisdom ideas that Isaiah knew well and which influenced him so strongly. Probably the most important contribution that Jensen makes is to show the broad base on which Isaiah's teaching really rests. Isaiah did receive his convictions about justice and community from the wisdom schools and training in which he was educated. But to this Isaiah added the powerful additional motivation of the holiness of God which was impressed on him in his inaugural vision.

Wisdom and Leaders

In discussing Isa 5:8–24, Jensen says,

Those here addressed, i.e., the royal officials, function both as advisers to the king and as administrators of justice. As men who have been educated in the school which undoubtedly existed in Jerusalem for the training of scribes for the royal court and of children of the upper classes, those who were destined for careers at court, they had been introduced into all the riches of the wisdom tradition and could lay claim to belonging to the circle of the wise. Isaiah accuses them of being poor advisers, of being corrupt judges, and of neglecting the ideals of their training, the value of which he does not question.[25]

Going beyond specific passages in which Isaiah exhibits wisdom influence, Jensen suggests that Isaiah may even have played a role in helping the wisdom tradition achieve the insight that true wisdom comes from God.[26] Isaiah was indeed a prophet, but his ties with wisdom are striking.[27]

Notes

1. Scandinavian scholarship emphasized this possibility. See, for example, Johannes Pedersen, "The Role Played by Inspired Persons among the Israelites and the Arabs," *Studies in Old Testament Prophecy,* (FS Theodore H. Robinson; Edinburgh: T. & T. Clark, 1946) 127–42 or A. R. Johnson, *The Cultic Prophet in Ancient Israel* (2d ed.; Cardiff: University of Wales, 1962).

2. Jer 1:1, "The words of Jeremiah, the son of Hilkiah, of the priests who were in Anathoth in the land of Benjamin." "If this is correct, it means that Jeremiah could claim as proud a lineage as any man in Israel, for he could, through Abiathar, boast of descent from none other than the house of Eli, . . . the priests who had been custodians of the Ark at Shilo," John Bright, *Jeremiah* (AB; Garden City: Doubleday, 1965) lxxxviii.

3. Ezek 1:3, "The word of the Lord came to Ezekiel the priest, the son of Buzi, in the land of the Chaldeans by the river Chebar." "His interest in the temple, his knowledge of sacral ordinances, as well as the closeness of his language to that of the Code of Holiness and the Priestly Document, provide sufficient external support for this," Walther Zimmerli, *Ezekiel* (Hermeneia; Philadelphia: Fortress, 1979) 1:16.

4. H. W. Wolff, *Amos the Prophet* (Philadelphia: Fortress, 1973).

5. These differences exist along with the similarities between Amos and Isaiah that appear in Rienhard Fey, *Amos und Jesaja* (Neukirchen-Vluyn: Neukirchener, 1963).

6. "We would expect to find him among the higher ranks of society there [in Jerusalem]. Only such a station as this could account for his freedom of intercourse with the king or with high officials," Gerhard von Rad, *Old Testament Theology* (Harper & Row, 1965) 2: 147. But cf. "The only explicit indication of Isaiah's relationship with the court is that he had to accost Ahaz while the king was (apparently) inspecting the water supply of Jerusalem (7:3). If anything, this implies the *in*accessibility of the court to

Isaiah," J. M. Ward, "Isaiah," *Interpreter's Dictionary of the Bible, Supplementary Volume* (Nashville: Abingdon, 1976) 457.

7. Robert T. Anderson, "Was Isaiah a Scribe?" *JBL* 79 (1960) 57–58.

8. Cf. André Lemaire, *Les écoles et la formation de la Bible dans l'ancient Israël* (Orbis biblicus et orientalis 39; Fribourg, 1981).

9. William McKane, *Prophets and Wise Men* (Studies in Biblical Theology 44; London: SCM, 1965) 115 n. 1, calls this idea "fanciful."

10. J. Fichtner, "Jesaja unter den Weisen," *TLZ* 74 (1949) cols. 75–80.

11. Johannes Lindblom, "Wisdom in the Old Testament Prophets," *SVT* 3 (1960) 192–204.

12. Some examples would be the Edomites in Jer 49:7, the Phoenicians in the figure of the King of Tyre in Ezek 28, and the Egyptians in Isa 19:11. Despite the wisdom of others, Jer 10:7 affirms that Israel's God is incomparable even to their achievements.

13. Besides Jer 18:18, see Jer 9:23 (Hebrew 9:22), "Let not the wise man glory in his wisdom, let not the mighty man glory in his might, let not the rich man glory in his riches."

14. William McKane, *Prophets and Wise Men*, as in note 9 above.

15. McKane bases his analysis of von Rad on the latter's "Die ältere Weisheit Israels," *Kerygma und Dogma* 2 (1956) 54–72 and "Josephgeschichte und ältere Chokma," *SVT* 1 (1953) 120–27. Von Rad later published *Wisdom in Israel* (Nashville: Abingdon, 1973).

16. William J. Whedbee, *Isaiah and Wisdom* (New York: Abingdon, 1971).

17. Ibid., 65–66.

18. Brevard S. Childs had identified this form in *Isaiah and the Assyrian Crisis* (SBT, 2d Series; London: SCM, 1967).

19. In the KJV of Isa 1–39, the word "Woe" occurs at 3:9, 11; 5:8, 11, 18, 20, 21, 22; 6:5 (Isaiah to himself); 10:1; 17:12; 18:1; 24:16; 28:1; 29:1, 15; 30:1; 31:1; 33:1.

20. E. Gerstenberger, "The Woe-Oracles of the Prophets,"

JBL 81 (1962) 249–63 and *Wesen und Herkunft des "apodiktischen Rechts"* (WMANT 20; Neukirchen-Vluyn: Neukirchener, 1965).

21. Hans-Jürgen Hermisson, "Weisheit und Geschichte," in *Probleme Biblischer Theologie* (FS G. von Rad; Munich: Chr. Kaiser, 1971) 136–54.

22. The classic study on Isaiah and history is Hans Wildberger, "Jesajas Verständnis der Geschichte," *SVT* 9 (1963) 83–117.

23. Joseph Jensen, *The Use of tôrâ by Isaiah: His Debate with the Wisdom Tradition* (CBQMS 3; Washington, DC: The Catholic Biblical Association, 1973).

24. Joseph Jensen, *Isaiah 1–39* (Old Testament Message 8; Wilmington: Michael Glazier, 1984).

25. Ibid., 79.

26. Ibid., 132. The biblical references are Prov 8:1–9:11 and Sirach 1:1, 5–7.

27. Biblical scholarship rarely allows a position to go unchallenged. J. Vermeylen, "Le Proto-Isaïe et la sagesse d'Israël," in *La Sagesse de l'Ancien Testament* (BETL 51; Gembloux: J. Duculot, 1979) 39–58, has denied that one can see anything of the wisdom establishment in Isaiah. "Les paroles 'authentiques' du prophète n'offrent que des contacts superficiels avec la sagesse israélite, explicables par la formation intellectuelle d'Isaie et par auditoire cultivé auquel il s'adressait," 57.

6.

Isaiah: Doom

The prophets of Israel have sometimes been depicted exclusively as persons called by God to warn the people of coming disaster.[1] Although this view of Israel's prophets has often been challenged and corrected, some scholars continue to view a given prophet in this way. Such a view claims Isaiah as a prophet of doom, and this position argues that this depiction of Isaiah is the accurate way for seeing this prophet of Jerusalem in the eighth century BCE.

Isaiah was not the first prophet of doom. He belongs to the group of four prophets of the eighth century who together form a chorus of doom. And well they should. Conditions, at least according to them, were bad and getting worse. Some people suffered excruciating need while others rested on their ivory beds.

> Woe to those who lie upon beds of ivory,
>   and stretch themselves upon their couches.
>
> Amos 6:4

Some went to market without shoes while others drank wine and lived in luxury.

> Woe to those . . . who drink wine in bowls,
>   and anoint themselves with the finest oils.
>
> Amos 6:6

Amos saw the situation and came with a message of doom. He preached that the kingdom of Samaria would fall as a result of its social injustice. And it did. Hosea decried the religious life of the same northern kingdom, and he too saw a disaster coming. Although Hosea seems to foresee a time of restoration, he declared that the North's coming purgation would be severe. Micah preached in the southern kingdom. His message was no less a doom-filled one. He condemned the seizing of property and the oppression of people. He preached the end of Jerusalem.

This is the group Isaiah joined. But there is something of a surprise in suggesting that Isaiah was a prophet of doom. Despite the fact that some prophets before Amos spoke words of judgment against individual persons, the role of the prophet in relation to the king and people was often one of consolation and support. Thus, at the time of Jeremiah there were many "peace prophets."

> They have healed the wound of my people lightly,
>   saying, "Peace, peace,"
>   when there is no peace.[2]
>
> Jer 6:14 and 8:11

In addition, Jerusalem, the hometown of Isaiah, may well have had a way of viewing itself as the city that could not be captured, for God had made this city his chosen place of dwelling. If this tradition of security did thrive in the city, Isaiah by his preaching of judgment and punishment would be going against a long-standing mentality, a tradition of Zion's protection against any threat of outside attack.[3]

Disaster

J. Vermeylen sees the message of Isaiah as basically one of doom.[4] The prophet is to warn the people. But he knows that nothing is likely to avert the coming catastrophe. The corruption and sinfulness has become too great, the infidelity too blatant, the unbelief too willful. Disaster was virtually inevitable. Isaiah warned the people that punishment was on its way, so that they, when punishment came, would have this one last chance, though it too, in all likelihood, would be rejected.[5]

Isaiah saw God's promises of security as conditional. No one is pleasing to God simply by being chosen by God. One must respond to God in fidelity and within oneself. The interior of a person is what counts with God. There is no magic in Isaiah's approach to religion. The promise is not something to hide behind. The covenant is not an automatic guarantee of perpetual favor but a call to responsibility. In the service of the true God, there can be no half-heartedness and no escape.

Because of this, Isaiah did not have that much interest in simply rehearsing the acts of God. The well-performed cult could honor the past to packed assemblies, but Isaiah was not interested. When he says

> Add year to year
>   let the feasts run their round,
>
> Isa 29:1

he is speaking ironically. Isaiah surely knew that God had chosen Zion as his dwelling, but he did not rely blindly on the presence of God in Zion. He knew that while some people depended on this guarantee, real security lay in a moral response to a moral God.

Isaiah put his trust in Yahweh. He alone could save his people from their enemies. He who held the world in his control surely would guard this chosen people if only they would act as they should. It was the leaders of the people who had led them astray, with the result that the people abandoned the way of God. Punishment and destruction was the inevitable consequence of such action.

Vermeylen sees Isaiah himself as an extraordinary religious figure, a man haunted by the reality of the divine. Isaiah saw God in his mystery in the temple vision. From then on—or better, even before that, since Isa 6 does not represent the initial call to the prophetic role according to Vermeylen[6]—Isaiah experiences the holiness of God as that which demands all from a person and from his people.

Invasion

Those who raged against Israel are easily under the control of Yahweh. These he would conquer, as he had done in times past when Israel took the land. But the provision is that Israel would have to live up to its calling and make the response that God expected. Isaiah is fully aware of this, and because of the sin of the people, he preached the invasion of Israel by the peoples of the East. And almost in confirmation of his message, the North fell during Isaiah's career. In just over a century the South was doomed to follow suit. Even before Isaiah's death, the South suffered a massive foreign invasion.

Isaiah certainly knew of the military ambitions and arrogant self-reliance of the leaders of the people. They depended on and trusted in their own carefully developed strength. They looked not to Yahweh but to their own interests and their own accomplishments. They had traditions of God's choice and continued care. They preferred to assume that these were given unconditionally, that nothing beyond the knowledge of and the invoking of those privileges would be required.

To the leaders who were so wrapped up in themselves Isaiah preached a Yahweh who placed different kinds of demands on them from those of simple conformity and complacency. Yahweh, the all holy, cannot be fooled by exterior worship.

> This people draw near with their mouth
>   and honor me with their lips,
>   while their hearts are far from me,
> and their fear of me is a commandment of men
>   learned by rote.
>
> Isa 29:13

He sees injustice, decries oppression, judges the leaders, and hence must punish.

> It is you who have devoured the vineyard,
>   the spoil of the poor is in your houses.

What do you mean by crushing my people,
    by grinding the face of the poor?

Isa 3:14–15

Yahweh is not a god who can be manipulated. All persons, including the leaders, can truly respond to Yahweh only in purity
of heart. And instead of this, Judah's leaders offered hardened
hearts and stupid actions, and they chose not to turn to the God
who saves those who truly serve him.

Memoirs as Witness

The real thrust of Isaiah's purpose should be clear from an
examination of the memoirs of Isaiah (Isa 6:1–9:6). Vermeylen
accepts the standard view that these memoirs were written relatively early in Isaiah's years of prophetic ministry.[7] Vermeylen
emphasizes that the book of Isaiah grew and developed over the
centuries, not by chance growth and haphazard additions, but by
fresh understandings and radical adaptations of the prophetic
words to new situations. The memoirs were the beginning of that
development.

For Vermeylen, chapters 6, 7, and 8 contain some shorter,
authentic sayings that were later brought together to form a collection. Thus 6:1–10, 7:4–9, 11–17, 8:1–4, 6–8, 11–15, 16–18
had been separate words or sayings of Isaiah which he or possibly
someone close to him combined as his memoirs. Over the years,
these words were expanded by clarifications and additions, and
this expansion during the centuries produced the present text.
The chant of Isa 8:23b–9:6 was composed during the time of the
exile as a fitting conclusion to this collection of Isaiah's sayings.

A close analysis of chapter 6 shows that this is not a text about
Isaiah's first prophetic encounter with God. One reason for this
claim is that narratives about a person's initial call to the service
of God generally do not put the emphasis on the willingness of the
one who is called, as does Isa 6. This chapter narrates an experience of Isaiah that occurred sometime after he began his prophetic career. Within that experience, he spontaneously offers

himself as a spokesman to speak the words which Yahweh the King will give him.

The overwhelming presentation of God's power in chapter 6 does not record the beginning of Isaiah's response to God, but rather the immediate response of an already faithful servant. Nevertheless, the experience and the awe of this moment are so dynamic that they will nourish Isaiah's continued response to God from this moment throughout the rest of his life. This passage, with its power and awe, is the literary basis for Vermeylen's description of Isaiah as "haunted by the disaster which would overtake his people."[8]

The new mission Isaiah receives at this audience with the divine King of Israel is to preach to the people even though they will not respond.

> Make the heart of this people fat,
>   and their ears heavy,
>   and shut their eyes;
> lest they see with their eyes,
>   and hear with their ears,
> and understand with their hearts,
>   and turn and be healed.
>
> Isa 6:10

Vermeylen poses the question that people have often asked about the command given to Isaiah: How is this hardening of hearts and dulling of minds meant? How is Isaiah's activity to be understood?[9]

The solution, according to Vermeylen, is that disaster is on its way. The leaders of the people so led the people astray that conversion is most unlikely. Although judgment has already been pronounced against Israel, Isaiah's mission is to give the people one last chance for repentance and hence for salvation. A real paradox is present. The prophet is to open the eyes of Israel, show the people the gravity of their failure and the urgency of their need to be converted to God, yet the prophet's work will only result in confirming the blindness of the people and in bringing about their ruin.

Syro-Ephraimite War

Chapter 7 gives a concrete example of this. Isaiah approaches king Ahaz with the plea to trust Yahweh. This was more than a simple meeting of prophet and king. Ahaz was king of the southern kingdom, Judah, and he was getting pressure from the king of the northern kingdom, Israel.

Because all the prophets, and Isaiah in particular, usually addressed and were engaged in the political events of their day, a brief historical overview of the political situation is in order. Isaiah lived in the eighth century BCE, four centuries after the time of David. The empire that David set up did not last. David's son, Solomon, mistreated some of his subjects in the northern parts of his realm. The death of that monarch was the occasion for the North to protest the harsh treatment it had received from Solomon.

After the northern kingdom acquired its independence from the king in Jerusalem, the two kingdoms, now called Israel and Judah respectively, went to war numerous times. But occasionally the kings of Jerusalem lived in peace with the kings of the northern realm. In fact, in times of cooperation and collaboration, both kingdoms prospered. Such times occurred in the ninth century with the reigns of kings Jehoshaphat and Ahab and in the eighth century with those of Uzziah and Jeroboam II.

But such times of success and prosperity often became times of corruption and oppression. The eighth century prophets bear this out, as seen above. And now, early in Isaiah's career, the North sought the help of the South against Assyria who threatened political control.[10]

In this narrative of Isaiah's first meeting with Ahaz, the king does not speak at all. He simply is told by Isaiah,

Unless you believe, you will not remain.[11]

Isa 7:9

A second encounter with Ahaz shows without any mitigating words the king's lack of trust. Isaiah even promises the sign of his own son, Immanuel (God-with-us), in the face of Ahaz's refusal to trust (7:14).[12] This sign is a double sign: it is a threat of divine presence to bring punishment if there is no return to God; but if there is conversion, then the presence would bring salvation.

Isaiah's other son, Maher-Shalal-Hash-Baz, bears another symbolic name: Plunder-hastens-robbery-is-quick (8:1). In this name there is no ambiguity: the devastation will come. But this episode must be taken with the earlier narrative in which Ahaz is offered the chance to show his faith. Isaiah had pleaded with the king, and the king had refused. So too Isaiah spoke to the people, and in their refusal, their own blindness is revealed.

Isaiah had completed his task. He had preached to king and people and now he can end his career. He withdraws from public activity, leaving only the memory of himself and his sons for that public (whom he, perhaps contemptuously, calls "this people") as a reminder that God had spoken and threatened the disaster and they would not respond. The king does not believe and the leaders do not trust in Yahweh. But Isaiah believes and trusts.

> Bind up the testimony, seal the teaching among my disciples. I will wait for the Lord, who is hiding his face from the house of Jacob, and I will hope in him. Behold, I and the children whom the Lord has given me are signs and portents in Israel from the Lord of hosts, who dwells on Mount Zion.
>
>   Isa 8:16–18

Isaiah knows that Yahweh will accomplish his plans from his abode on Mount Zion.

In Vermeylen's view, this collection—the vision in chapter 6 and the narratives in chapters 7 and 8—was probably brought together by the prophet himself shortly after the Syro-Ephraimite war. In the next century, the collection was edited during the reign of Manasseh. The purpose of this edition of the collection was to refocus the threats, which originally had been made against the people of God in Judah and which now were made to apply to the Northern Kingdom. This, of course, was done to emphasize the power of the prophetic word, for the Northern Kingdom had actually fallen in the eighth century. This work showed that Isaiah had predicted that fall.

Modification of Tradition

This refocusing of the threats allowed for the introduction of the idea of the inviolability of Zion.[13] For in 701 the armies of the Assyrian emperor Sennacherib had come to Jerusalem but withdrew before serious damage could be done to the city. The glorification of this event was a major aspect of the editing of this collection of Isaiah's words. Thus, the threat of Immanuel, God present to punish, became the promise of Immanuel, God present to protect. The doom which had been predicted by Isaiah now became expectation of security. A new generation found new hope in the words of Isaiah.

The collection of Isaiah's words, which now are contained within 6:1–8:18, was not the only collection of his utterances. Another collection (parts of 2:12–3:24) spoke of humbling the proud and of the exaltation of Yahweh. A third collection hurled "woes" against pride and social injustice (most of 5:8–23 and 10:1–3). A dramatic sequence of events by which Yahweh tried to break the pride of this people forms the fourth collection (9:7–20 + 5:24–29). The remaining collection is one of "woes" directed against those who lack confidence in Yahweh in the foreign affairs of Judah (10:5–14 + 14:24–25 + 18:1–4 + 28:1–4 + 29:1–4 + 30:1–5 + 31:1–3 + 33:1).[14]

This approach of Vermeylen sees these independent collections coming together gradually, reaching their present shape by the time of Josiah in the late seventh century. Some passages were added that spoke explicitly about Josiah. Thus, Isa 9:1–6 was written about Josiah, not as a prediction of some future great king, but to express the hopes of the people that this king would truly live up to the expectations that the Davidic dynasty held and that had not yet been fulfilled.

Vermeylen's view of Isaiah as a prophet of doom is accomplished by dating many of the more optimistic passages in Isaiah

1–35 to a date later than Isaiah himself. This method does not allow the city traditions of Jerusalem to influence the prophet a great deal. But it does set him firmly among the other eighth century prophets who foresaw catastrophe. Isaiah, then, stands indeed as a prophet of doom, one who preached the fall of his own people.

Notes

1. In order for anyone to make this assertion, that person has to ignore the prophetic passages that are not doom-filled. As chapter 1 above showed, this assessment is often done by declaring such passages to be inauthentic, that is, not from the prophet himself. Bernhard Duhm, in his commentary on Isaiah, *Das Buch Jesaja* (1st ed., 1892) excluded many passages from authentic Isaiah on a literary basis, namely, he supposed that the authentic words of the prophet were always in poetic form and that the prophet never spoke in simple prose.

2. In his personal dispute with the prophet Hananiah, Jeremiah claimed, "The prophets who preceded you and me from ancient times prophesied war, famine, and pestilence against many countries and great kingdoms. As for the prophet who prophesies peace, when the word of that prophet comes to pass, then it will be known that the Lord has truly sent the prophet" (Jer 28:8–9).

3. This idea of the inviolability of Zion is one of the major elements in what has been called "The Zion Tradition." See J. J. M. Roberts, "Zion Tradition," *Interpreter's Dictionary of the Bible, Supplementary Volume,* 985–87, who includes this idea of inviolability under "The Conquest of Chaos." See also John H. Hayes, "The Tradition of Zion's Inviolability," *JBL* 82 (1963) 419–26.

4. J. Vermeylen, *Du prophète Isaïe à l'apocalyptique: Isaïe I-XXXV, miroir d'un demi-millénaire d'expérience religieuse en Israël* (2 vols.; Paris: Gabalda, 1977–78). Vermeylen admits of a strictly limited use of the word "conversion" for the prophet's goal (2:667, n. 2). If the people could believe, the nation would survive. But the coming destruction, in reality, will have to be general (2:666). G. Sauer is a contemporary scholar who maintains the

picture of Isaiah as a complete doom prophet (as did some turn-of-the-century commentators, e.g., Duhm); see G. Sauer, "Die Umkehrforderung in der Verkündigung Jesajas," in *Wort-Gebot-Glaube* (FS W. Eichrodt, AThANT 59; Zurich, 1970).

5. Ibid., 2:659–71.

6. Those who held that position before Vermeylen include M. M. Kaplan, "Isaiah 6:1–11," *JBL* 45 (1926) 251–59; F. Hesse, *Das Verstockungsproblem im Alten Testament* (BZAW 74; Berlin, 1955) 84–85; J. Milgrom, "Did Isaiah prophesy during the Reign of Uzziah?" *VT* 14 (1964) 164–82.

7. Karl Budde proposed that Isaiah 6 and 7 are part of a work he called the "Memoirs of Isaiah," *Jesaja's Erleben: Eine gemeinverständliche Auslegung der Denkschrift des Propheten (Kap 6,1–9,6)* (Gotha: Klotz, 1928).

8. Vermeylen, 661.

9. Many have pondered the problem of the hardening of the heart in Isaiah and in the Old Testament in general. See the work of Hesse in note 6 above, that of G. von Rad on Isaiah in *Old Testament Theology* 2:151–55, and Rudolf Kilian, *Jesaja 1–39* (Erträge der Forschung; Darmstadt: Wissenschaftliche Buchgesellschaft, 1983).

10. This military and political crisis of the two kingdoms has often been called, although there has been criticism of the name, "the Syro-Ephraimite War." Two recent studies on it are Michael E. W. Thompson, *Situation and Theology: Old Testament Interpretations of the Syro-Ephraimite War* (Sheffield: Almond, 1982) and Jesús Maria Asurmendi, *La guerra siro-efraimita: Historia y profetas* (Valencia/Jerusalem: Edilvia, 1982).

11. The Hebrew of these words reads " 'im lo' ta'amînû, kî lo' te'amenû." Sheldon H. Blank, *Prophetic Faith in Isaiah* (Detroit: Wayne State University, 1967) 18, understands the Hebrew as a repetition of the first choice that Ahaz could make, "If you will not believe, then ask a sign." The two ways that the words "if you will not believe" (lo' ta'aminu and lo' te'amenu) were both recorded in the text eventually were not seen as two alternative readings but as a full conditional sentence.

12. The identity (and parents) of Immanuel has, of course, been much debated. Joseph Jensen, *Isaiah 1–39* (Old Testament

Message 8; Wilmington: Michael Glazier, 1984) 96–97, treats the question whether Isaiah was referring to Jesus of Nazareth. For a review of much of the discussion see any of the commentaries or R. Kilian, *Jesaja 1–39*, 12–26.

13. The position of Vermeylen, thus, is quite far from the view that sees the prophet Isaiah convinced of the inviolability of Zion, a view which appears in other interpretations of Isaiah treated later in this book.

14. A later chapter of this book will give details of this position and will mention some of the other ways of viewing the development of the collection.

7.

Isaiah: Conversion

Not all biblical scholars read Isaiah mainly as a prophet of doom. Isaiah's situation was indeed depressing: in the midst of a sinful people who had to be punished, Isaiah was commanded to announce that a catastrophe was coming. But did God really have no other idea for his people than destruction?[1]

Georg Fohrer sees all the prophets as preachers of repentance and conversion. The prophet is one who speaks to the people in the name of God that they might return to God—that they might recognize their sin, turn to their Lord, and begin again to live in a relationship with the God who called them. Isaiah does in his day what Amos did in his, Hosea in his, and later on what Jeremiah and Ezekiel would do in theirs.[2]

Repentance and conversion, in Fohrer's view, are the dominant themes of the preaching of Isaiah throughout his career with its varied moments and insights. Fohrer identifies four periods of Isaiah's prophetic activity.[3] The first period, 740–736, began with his inaugural vision, chapter 6. The Syro-Ephraimite war, 735–733, was the second period.[4]

The third period, 716–711, began some five years after the fall of the northern kingdom to the Assyrians. These early years of Hezekiah's reign saw the attempted revolt against Assyria which was instigated by the Philistines and the Egyptians. The final period, 705–701, culminated in Sennacherib's invasion of Judah and his siege of Jerusalem. A major new insight and orientation occurred at the beginning of three of these periods: the first, the second, and the fourth.[5]

Changing Insights

When Isaiah was called in his inaugural vision, the first period of Isaiah's prophetic ministry began.[6] The overwhelming experience of the inaugural vision convinced Isaiah that Yahweh was changing his attitude to Israel. Isaiah would now cease warning and coaxing his people and their leaders who were obstinate in their sins. Yahweh decided that judgment would soon come upon the leaders of this people. Utter defeat and annihilation was coming from God to those about whom Isaiah cried,

> O my people,
> your leaders mislead you,
> and confuse the course of your paths.
>
> Isa 3:12[7]

Israel can no longer count simply on God's non-judgmental protection and salvation. In fact, neither Israel the people as a whole nor the individual Israelite lives simply in a condition of salvation or a condition of non-salvation. Isaiah called people out of the traditional securities and platitudes into a new kind of responsible existence. This was truly a major change from the assurance and consolation within which Isaiah and his contemporaries had been born and nurtured.

Another major change in Isaiah's approach to things occurred when he met king Ahaz during the Syro-Ephraimite war in the second period of his prophetic activity. The northern kingdom wanted to force Judah into rebellion with Israel and Damascus against the empire of the Assyrians.[8] Isaiah's goal was to elicit from Ahaz an act of trust in God. This act of trust would include a commitment to make no alliances with foreign powers, for such dealings would manifest a distrust toward God and his power.

In chapter 7, Isaiah encourages Ahaz to ask for a sign. In response to Ahaz's refusal to ask for a sign, God himself sends a sign. The sign will be the desolation and abandonment of the land. The birth of a child Immanuel is the preliminary movement toward the destruction, which is to be so complete that the people (and the child) will be reduced to the diet of nomads, "curds and honey" (7:15, 22).

> Therefore the Lord himself will give you a sign. Behold, a young woman shall conceive and bear a son, and shall call his name Immanuel. He shall eat curds and honey when he knows how to refuse the evil and choose the good. For before the child knows to refuse the evil and choose the good, the land before whose two kings you are in dread will be deserted.
>
> Isa 7:14–16

The consoling phrase "God is/will be with us" which formerly served as security now becomes a threat.

Isaiah's change of view that is connected with this second period of his prophetic ministry is the shift from the conviction that just the leaders will perish to the realization that the whole people would be punished. And that punishment would be grievous. The misfortune which is about to befall Israel is as great as the disaster of the division of the kingdom after the death of Solomon.

> The Lord will bring upon you and upon your people and upon your father's house such days as have not come since the day that Ephraim departed from Judah—the king of Assyria.
>
> Isa 7:17

From now on, Isaiah is to preach both the downfall of the leaders and the fall of the nation itself. The threat will take time to work itself out. But it is inevitable, if no change occurs.

Three words of Isaiah (14:28–32; 29:1–8; 31:4–9) from this time offer strong admonitions as a last faint hope for repentance.

> I would kill your root with famine,
>   and your remnant I might slaughter.
>
> Isa 14:30

Isaiah preached an announcement of disaster to come and a lament for the unwillingness of the people to be saved (30:15–17). Henceforth he could utter only a few calls for repentance while foreign nations would bring Yahweh's judgment on the people Israel.

The last change in Isaiah, a major new insight that appears in the final stage of his preaching, relates to the foreign powers that God had been using to bring judgment on his people. The Assyrians had been an instrument in the hand of Yahweh

> Ah, Assyria, the rod of my anger,
>   the staff of my fury!
>
>   Isa 10:5[9]

and this instrument Yahweh had wielded to accomplish his purpose, namely to punish the people for their sinful behavior. In Isaiah's first outlook, God sent prophets to turn the people to himself. In the prophet's second view, God used the other peoples to carry out his desire to prod Israel by military and political threats to return to him. This new third insight Isaiah acquired late in his career was that these people too, especially Assyria, would be punished by God for their pride and for their affronts against the God of Israel.

That Yahweh will destroy Assyria on his own land was a dramatic change of mind for the prophet. Assyria ultimately did not acknowledge the supremacy of Yahweh, and hence that nation had to fall. Isaiah perceived Yahweh's greatness and omnipotence already in his earliest vision. The perception grew so much during his prophetic career that it was no surprise for the prophet later in his life to see the divine logic by which, after using the Assyrians for his purpose, Yahweh would destroy them because of their own corruption and self-exaltation. Yahweh would bring Assyria against Judah in order to punish Judah, but Assyria itself must be defeated in Yahweh's own land.

> I will break the Assyrian in my land,
>   and upon my mountains trample him under foot.
>
>   Isa 14:25

Even so, this could not lessen the judgment against Judah.[10]

Isaiah never achieved the hope of redemption that Hosea, Jeremiah and Ezekiel eventually did. Even Amos and Micah had some word of hope—whether it was by the promise of a holy remnant, the promise of divine protection for Zion, or the hope of peace from the messianic ruler who would come. Isaiah had no hope to offer, and he ended his career with the following words that show no anticipation of anything better to come.

> The Lord of hosts has revealed himself in my ears:
> "Surely this iniquity will not be forgiven you
>   till you die."
>
> Isa 22:14

No hope appears here either:

> For the palace will be forsaken,
>   the populous city deserted;
> the hill and the watchtower
>   will become dens for ever,
> a joy of wild asses,
>   a pasture of flocks.
>
> Isa 32:14

Repentance

Fohrer believes that throughout Isaiah's life and through the various modifications of his views and the increasing insight regarding God's activity, Isaiah continued his work with one purpose in mind, to preach conversion and repentance. Although he understood that God was working in the national situation and political events of his day, Isaiah aimed his preaching at the individual and demanded that the individual turn to God in true service and whole-hearted religion.

Conversion for Isaiah was something interior, the orientation of a person that comes from within, from the person's spirit. Even religious actions are meaningless and worthless without the interior. This assessment applies directly to the cult, for, although he was aware of the ritual practice of Israel (as well as of the exterior religious actions of the non-Israelites), Isaiah never praised the cultic system of Israel. The prophet does not rely on sacrifice and external observance as the mark of true religion, because God looks to the heart.

Nor did Isaiah allow a person to depend for status and security on being a member of Israel, the people of God. One cannot just trust in the covenant. (Indeed, Fohrer agrees with those scholars who do not see the idea of covenant to be a major theological datum of ancient Israel until the Deuteronomic movement.)[11]

What God asks of his faithful one is "doing God's will in daily life."

> Cease to do evil,
>   learn to do good;
> seek justice,
>   correct oppression;
> defend the fatherless,
>   plead for the widow.

Isa 1:16–17

This means a faithful compliance to what God has revealed as his desire for his people. Israel's ethical tradition, community-oriented and compassionate for the powerless, is clear enough. And the prophet takes care to refer explicitly to it, namely, the removal of injustice and the protection of the less fortunate. This obedience must come from the heart, as true obedience can come from nowhere else.

Conversion means turning away from a glorified self. The individual must give up pride and self-reliance. One's reliance must be placed only in God. One must look to God for life, meaning, and security.[12] One cannot set up one's own meaning and order. These are given by God, revealed to human beings by God's messengers. If one responds to God in the present, if one chooses God and God's will, if one is changed by the preaching of conversion, then that person might become part of the remnant that will be saved. No pre-established boundaries determine who can become part of the remnant. "Even all Judah could be the 'remnant' that survives the terrible onslaughts of war."[13]

No Unqualified Salvation

To be sure, Isaiah gives no unconditional promise of salvation. Isaiah does not go along with any traditional assurance of security or divine favor. "The election tradition of standard Yahwism was destroyed for Isaiah at his call."[14] Nor can Fohrer find any "plan" for judgment and salvation. Fohrer rejects the usual translation—God's "plan"[15]—and offers God's "decision" instead, for the word refers to God's decision in an immediate concrete situation.

Fohrer is concerned not to restrict the will and decision of God by something from the past or by something from outside God. God is utterly free in his dealings with individuals. Likewise, the prophet is not limited to ideas from the past or by traditions that have been received from others. The prophet surveys the situation, hears the word of God in the present, responds using his rational faculties, and preaches the word of repentance to the sinful people.

Isaiah's long career made him an excellent example of one who could accommodate his message of conversion to the changing political situations and to the continuously developing insight he had into the divine purpose and action.

Fohrer's interpretation of Isaiah was carried further by Hans Werner Hoffmann.[16] Hoffmann accepts the standard description and analysis of the basic prophetic speech-form that consists of two parts, usually called the reproach and the threat.[17] In practice the form appears as this: "Because you have abandoned the way of the Lord, thus says Yahweh, the end is coming." Scholars have often suggested that the explanatory and prefatory words of the prophet ("because you have acted in this way") are the prophet's own analysis and are therefore not to be viewed as identified with or inseparable from the message of disaster which comes directly from God.

Hoffmann accepts this distinction even for Isaiah and his statements of a coming disaster, but he insists that an analysis of only the form does not necessarily reveal the true intention of the prophet. Isaiah's intention in preaching was to bring the people to conversion.

Conversion was Isaiah's constant and invariable goal throughout his ministry. Isaiah gave up this goal and its object, the people, only when Sennacherib's withdrawal from Jerusalem led to mindless rejoicing rather than to an inner conversion. Only then did he say,

> For the Lord has poured out upon you
>   a spirit of deep sleep,
> and has closed your eyes, the prophets,
>   and covered your heads, the seers.
>
> Isa 29:10

And ultimately,

> Surely this iniquity will not be forgiven you
>   till you die.
>
> Isa 22:14

Turning Back

The largest and most detailed commentary in contemporary biblical scholarship also depicts Isaiah as a preacher of repentance, one who warns his people of the consequences of their actions. Hans Wildberger agrees that Isaiah does not see God as irrevocably set on destroying his people.[18] Not some freak of fortune is going to happen, but the result of the people's response to God. If the people must be punished, it is because of their own choice to disobey the divine will.

True, Isaiah is not recorded as crying "Repent!" There is no imperative form of the verb *šwb* among the words of Isaiah.[19] A form of the verb occurs with God as the subject, "For all that, he did not turn back his anger" (Isa 5:23, 9:11, 16, 20; 10:4). The point there is that God would have "turned back" if the people would have "turned back" (repented, been converted).

The saying in 30:15, "in turning (back) . . . you shall be saved." There could hardly be any clearer assurance that security is possible than this saying—security, if one cooperates with God. Isaiah's son's name should not be forgotten, Shear-yashub, "a remnant shall (re)turn" (6:10).

For Wildberger, too, Isaiah pleads with the people to observe and to change their behavior. Isaiah is not simply a peace/salvation prophet; nor simply a doom prophet. He is one who warns the people.[20]

For this approach, Isaiah, even with all his emphasis on Jerusalem and all his connection with its kings, resembles and mirrors the other classical prophets. He too is a preacher of repentance.

Notes

1. One thinks of the words from a later time in Jer 29:11, "For I know the plans I have for you, says the Lord, plans for welfare and not for evil, to give you a future and a hope."

2. "[The prophets'] central theme is therefore the either/or of man's destruction or deliverance, though this does not make them simply preachers of repentance. The call to conversion points to a possibility of deliverance; this is the sum and substance of [their] preaching," Ernst Sellin and Georg Fohrer, *Introduction to the Old Testament* (New York: Abingdon, 1968) 346. Fohrer has published a commentary on Isaiah, *Das Buch Jesaja* (3 vols., Zürcher Bibelkommentare; Zürich: Zwingli, 1960, 1962, 1964; 2d ed vol 1, 1966, vol 2, 1967).

3. There are other ways of viewing Isaiah's ministry and finding periods of activity. For example, Otto Kaiser sees five periods in Isaiah's active life: (1) before 734, (2) 734–733, the Syro-Ephraimite War, (3) 733–722, to the fall of the northern kingdom, (4) 721–711, when the Philistines were fomenting revolt, (5) 705–701, to the deliverance of Jerusalem, *Introduction to the Old Testament: A Presentation of its Results and Problems* (Minneapolis: Ausburg, 1975) 22.

4. On the Syro-Ephraimite war, see the preceding chapter.

5. Georg Fohrer, "Wandlungen Jesajas," in *Festschrift Wilhelm Eilers* (Wiesbaden: Otto Harrassowitz, 1967) 58–71; repr in *Studien zu alttestamentlichen Texten und Themen (1966–1072)* (BZAW 155; Berlin: Walter de Gruyter, 1081) 11 23.

6. The date is given in Isa 6:1 as "the year that Uzziah died." Usually this is identified as 742 BCE.

7. One may note in passing that the first half of this verse (Isa 3:12) in the RSV needs correction: "My people—children are their oppressors and women rule over them." The NEB translates, with a very slight change in the Hebrew but in conformity with the Greek, "Money-lenders strip my people bare, and usurers lord it over them." This is preferable in the context, and it does not force one to the odd reasoning that is otherwise required to defend the verse against the charge of anti-feminism (for to equate the rule of a woman with disaster is neither fair nor historical). With this way of translating an emended text, there is no need to defend the RSV of Isa 3:12 by the following reasoning: "Isaiah was predicting chaos when a child still governed by its mother occupied the throne," John H. Otwell, *And Sarah Laughed: The Status of Women in the Old Testament* (Philadelphia: Westminster, 1977) 140.

8. For further details of the Syro-Ephraimite war, see the previous chapter.

9. The "hand" in the Hebrew of v 5 is grammatically a problem. The KJV reads v 5b literally, "and the staff in their hand is mine indignation;" while the RSV relegates "in their hand," to a marginal note. Vermeylen, *Du prophète*, 254–55, considers the word (in English it is translated by a phrase) an addition. Fohrer, 1:153, translates, "it is in my hand," but also considers it an addition. John Mauchline, *Isaiah 1–39*, (TBP; London: SCM, 1962) 122, explains that "hand" can mean "power" and suggests the meaning, "the staff empowered to convey my fury," pointing out that "the Assyrians are not wielding Yahweh's fury, but he is wielding the Assyrians as the staff of his fury."

10. Fohrer, 1:201.

11. Sellin-Fohrer, 373; *Jesaja*, 1:13.

12. *Jesaja*, 2:103.

13. Sellin-Fohrer, 373.

14. Ibid., 373 n 34.

15. One should note how important this word is for those who emphasize the influence of the wisdom tradition on Isaiah; cf. J. Fichtner, "Jahves Plan in der Botschaft des Jesaja," *ZAW* 63 (1951) 16–33.

16. Hans Werner Hoffmann, *Die Intention der Verkündigung Jesajas* (BZAW 136; Berlin: Walter de Gruyter, 1974).

17. See especially Claus Westermann, *Basic Forms of Prophetic Speech* (Philadelphia: Westminster, 1967).

18. Hans Wildberger, *Jesaja* (3 vols., BK; Neukirchen-Vluyn: Neukirchener, 1965–82). Wildberger's orientation was already evident in his article "Das Thema 'Umkehr' in der alttestamentliche Prophetie," *ZTK* 48 (1951) 129–48.

19. The translations for this Hebrew verb include "turn, return, repent, be converted." See William Holladay, *The Root Šubh in the Old Testament* (Leiden: E. J. Brill, 1958).

20. Wildberger, *Jesaja*, 3:1643.

8.

Isaiah: Covenant

The idea of covenant has always played a major role in the interpretation of the Bible.[1] John Bright focuses on this concept in his interpretation of the preaching of Isaiah.[2] Bright begins, as many other scholars begin their analyses of this prophet, with the awareness that Isaiah's preaching centers on Jerusalem and David. Jerusalem was the center of the religious life of the people, but it was also their historical and political capital. Since the covenant was a historical experience, it is appropriate that Isaiah referred to it in certain historical settings.

Isaiah preached at the time when Assyria was regaining its power and now had expansionistic plans which threatened Judah and Israel. At the same time northern Israel formed an alliance with Syria to protect themselves against Assyria.[3] Isaiah saw this action of Israel only as infidelity and misplaced trust. In the face of all the political and military uncertainty, Isaiah preached trust in a God who would remain true to the promises he had made to Jerusalem and to the Davidic dynasty in the covenant he had given to David.

Trust

Chapters 6–8 of Isaiah refer to the rebellion of northern Israel and Syria against Assyria, the world empire of that day. From these texts Bright demonstrates that trust is a major concern of Isaiah. On the occasion of that rebellion, Isaiah tells the king in Jerusalem that the kings of both Syria and Samaria have their allotted tasks and powers. Isaiah refers to them as these two smoldering stumps of firebrands

Isa 7:4

and thereby shows that he has no fear of them. Then God says,

It shall not stand,
    and it shall not come to pass,

Isa 7:7

indicating the divine view of this proposed rebellion. The implication is that the Davidic king in Jerusalem has Yahweh and his promise behind him. All that is needed is belief.

If you will not believe,
    surely you will not be established.

Isa 7:9a

If this faith is lacking, disaster will overtake them.

Later, during the early reign of Hezekiah (714–712), there was another rebellion against Assyria, this one led by Ashdod and backed by Egypt. Judah had the same chance as before to seek freedom from Assyria by trust in the use of military might. Isaiah once again opposed rebellion against Assyria, because such action implied a lack of trust in the God who reigns on Zion. Indeed, the word to the representatives of the rebelling peoples is clear,

What will one answer the messengers of the nation?
"The Lord has founded Zion,
    and in her the afflicted of his people find refuge."

Isa 14:32

Isaiah called for trust even in the most trying situations.

Such an event was Sennacherib's attack against the city of Jerusalem in 701. Isaiah's message then as always was that one should place trust only in Yahweh and not in armaments. Despite the massive threat that Assyria raised, Yahweh was all the more trustworthy.

> In returning and rest
>> you shall be saved;
> in quietness and trust
>> shall be your strength.

Isa 30:15

The later narratives about the prophet carry a comparable message in this divine saying:

> I will protect this city and save it,
> for my own sake and my servant David's sake.

Isa 37:35[4]

Covenants

Isaiah based his assurance regarding the security of Jerusalem and the royal line on the covenant God had made with David. Bright explains that within certain groups the Sinaitic covenant (the covenant mediated by Moses on Mount Sinai), which constituted the formative and normative basis of the existence of Israel, was being pushed aside in favor of the Davidic covenant.[5] The Davidic covenant made for more comfortable living, as it were, because it did not allow for an end to God's favor toward his people.[6]

Bright discusses the theory that "covenant" was a relatively late idea in Israelite thought, a concept fully enunciated only by the Deuteronomistic school that flourished in the seventh century BCE. Bright weighs and discards this position. He claims that Isaiah knew the Sinaitic covenant traditions, even though the prophet did not refer to them explicitly.

Isaiah's tack and accomplishment in this competition between the two conceptions of covenant, the Sinaitic and the Davidic, was to qualify the one by the other. The Sinaitic covenant was a covenant with demands and stipulations by which Israel might remain Yahweh's people. The covenant to David was a promise of enduring support of his dynasty, even if Yahweh would have to punish and chastise some of the occupants of the throne (see Isa 89:29–37). The Davidic covenant seemed to understate the obligations that Israel had toward Yahweh and his will, namely, of "righteous behavior in accordance with this will under threat of his extreme displeasure."[7]

Isaiah saw the sins of Israel, and he knew that punishment was surely to come. The nation was to undergo a terrible catastrophe. Assyria would be God's instrument to discipline the people for their infidelity and pride.

> Ah, Assyria, the rod of my anger,
>   the staff of my fury!
> Against a godless nation I send him,
>   and against the people of my wrath I command him.
>
> Isa 10:5–6

But this chastisement, terrible though it would be, would not be the annihilation of the people. The disaster would serve to purge the people and to redirect them, even to reeducate them in a purer service to Yahweh.

Because of this moral and religious demand, which seems to flow from the Sinaitic covenant, Isaiah saw a future for the purified remnant. This promise of a remnant is dramatically presented in the name of Isaiah's son, Shear-yashub ("a remnant will return"). The ambiguity of the name suggests the duality within Isaiah's expectation. The name may imply that *only* a remnant will come back. But, on the other hand, the name may be taken to mean that a remnant will *surely* return to God in sorrow and faithful trust. Isaiah seems to have

> cherished the hope that each successive catastrophe that befell his nation would prove to be the needed discipline that would impel at least the best of this people to turn to their God in penitence and trust.[8]

Only if such repentance occurred, would salvation be a possibility.

Bright does not see Isaiah as preaching the inviolability of the city. Indeed, Bright seems not to envision a lively tradition about the inviolable city in Jerusalem during the time of Isaiah.[9] The inviolability of Zion, proposed by others as the basis for the false security at the time of Isaiah, does not form part of Bright's understanding of the prophet and his times. He thinks more easily of the election of the city and the election of the dynasty as the crucial elements of that complacency.

Bright has proposed that the conviction about Zion's inviolability is something that developed from the miraculous deliverance of the city when it had been attacked by Sennacherib. Bright dates this deliverance somewhat later than 701. He upholds the theory that Sennacherib led two campaigns to the West during the reign of Hezekiah. The story of the miraculous deliverance of the city, a tradition which really contradicts the defeat of 701, must be founded on a real event which came to pass after the event of 701.[10]

The Future

The Davidic covenant furnishes Isaiah with his vision for the future. Just as Yahweh had given David the power to defeat the Philistines and to establish Jerusalem as the capital city of his people, so will Yahweh send a royal redeemer figure. Isaiah's depiction is clearest in two different passages.

The first passage, 9:2–7 (numbering in the Hebrew text 9:1–6), appears in the form of "a dynastic hymn or oracle" that would be appropriate to the day of the royal crowning. "The piece is to read as a promise of future salvation."[11] In that future time, God's savior will be victorious, more victorious even than all the battles that Israel had to fight in the ancient past.

> For to us a child is born,
>   to us a son is given;
> and the government will be upon his shoulder,
>   and his name will be called,
> 'Wonderful Counselor, Mighty God,
>   Everlasting Father, Prince of Peace.'
>
> Isa 9:6

At that time there will be no more need for war and fighting. Justice and righteousness will abound under the rule of God's new man on the throne of David. This savior figure that Isaiah looked forward to was not simply a projection from "the hopes that the populace may have been led to repose in the dynasty through the affirmations of the official cult."[12] He would be a totally new experience.[13]

The second passage, 11:1–9, further clarifies the royal person. The

> messianic figure Isaiah describes was to be endowed
> with the divine spirit, "the spirit of wisdom and under-
> standing, the spirit of counsel and might, the spirit of
> knowledge and the fear of Yahweh" (11:2).[14]

Thus, Isaiah "stood in discontinuity with the existing order."[15]

> He shall not judge by what his eyes see,
>   or decide by what his ears hear;
> but with righteousness he shall judge the poor,
>   and decide with equity for the meek of the earth.
> > Isa 11:3–4

Beyond the chastisement that Yahweh had to send to his "faithless and rebellious nation, its rulers and its people" lay a time of fulfillment in which the royal redeemer would far surpass the glorious successes of David, because this person would bring about the actual divine rule on earth. This time of fulfillment would last forever; it would know no end.

Bright's understanding of the preaching of Isaiah, then, is more than simply modifying the Davidic covenant by the stipulations of the Sinaitic covenant. Bright underlines and possibly extends the spiritual hopes of the Davidic covenant in ancient Israel. It seems clear that Bright does not hesitate to read Isaiah from the perspective of a believing Christian, the spirit in which the New Testament writers read Isaiah.

Covenant In Other Words

Walter Eichrodt, the scholar who centered his famous *Theology of the Old Testament* on the idea of covenant,[16] wrote an article on Isaiah and covenant.[17] Eichrodt by no means considers the concept of covenant a late development in Israel's thought. Although some scholars have questioned the centrality of covenant for Isaiah's thought—in part because Isaiah does not use the Hebrew word for covenant, *berith*—Eichrodt explains Isaiah's relation to the covenant by several routes.

Isaiah does use terminology that reflects the close relation between Yahweh and Israel. The designation for God, "the Holy One of Israel" (1:4, 5:19, 24; 10:17; 29:19; 30:11, 12, 15; 31:1; 37:23) is first on the list of phrases that reveal Isaiah's covenant-people focus. The list also includes "Yahweh Sabaoth" and the simple designation "the God of Israel." So much is the prophet taken up with the ancient covenant relation that Isaiah can even call Judah, the southern kingdom, by the old name of the amphictyony, Israel.

Isaiah does not hesitate to attribute to God the familial relations of father and lover, terms often connected with treaty members. The reason why Zion can be spoken of in such magnificent imagery as "the centre of God's universal dominion," the goal of the pilgrimage of the nations, is that the Israelite traditions have taken up Zion into their realm and power. The God of Israel has chosen Jerusalem as his abode; no wonder that he will defend it. Eichrodt cites A. R. Johnson who shows that in the royal psalms "the Covenant with David presupposed here does not exclude the Sinai Covenant."[18]

Clearly, Isaiah, in this perspective, has the Sinai covenant in mind, but he does not use the word *berith*. Eichrodt explains that in the monarchic period there was prevalent the misunderstanding

> by which the covenant was seen in terms of the ordinary legal system: the fact that it had consolidated and hardened into a statutory relationship, providing mutual benefits for two equal partners, stood in sharp contrast to the

struggle of the prophets for an inward submission of the
people to Yahweh in personal love and trust.[19]

Although the Zion ideas were finding their place within the covenant with Israel, and although Isaiah made use of those Zion
concepts, nevertheless he could not use, because of its misuse,
the word "covenant," *berith*.[20]

But, Eichrodt feels, the condemnation of this corrupt society
clearly presupposes the covenant. Only the covenant with Israel
could account for Yahweh's judgment against the pride and injustice of all realms of society. And only the covenant could yet
hold out a promise of new beginnings after the catastrophe which
had to come.

Existence as a covenanted people—this is a way that scholars
have frequently proposed that ancient Israel understood itself. Although Isaiah does not mention Moses and Sinai, nevertheless,
certain scholars have read this prophet as a spokesman for the
covenant God, Yahweh. Thus, Isaiah is a prophet who calls the
people to the fidelity that is demanded by Israel's covenant with
Yahweh.

Notes

1. For surveys that treat covenant in Old Testament interpretation as a whole, see, among others, Gerhard Hasel, *Old Testament Theology: Basic Issues in the Current Debate* (3d rev ed;
Grand Rapids: Eerdmans, 1982) 117–19, and John H. Hayes and
Frederick Prussner, *Old Testament Theology: Its History and Development* (Atlanta: John Knox, 1985), "covenant" entry in the in-
dex.

2. John Bright, *Covenant and Promise: the Prophetic Understanding of the Future in Pre-exilic Israel* (Philadelphia:
Westminster, 1976) and Bright, "Isaiah," in *Peake's Commentary
on the Bible* (eds. M. Black and H. H. Rowley; London: Nelson,
1963).

3. Bright has written the most comprehensive single-au-
thored history of ancient Israel in English, *A History of Israel* (3d
ed; Philadelphia: Westminster, 1981). He treats "the Syro-

Ephraimite War" on pages 273–75 without using the term. Other scholars have pointed out the inappropriateness of the traditional term for this "very minor military undertaking," M. E. W. Thompson, *Situation and Theology* (see the references in the earlier chapter on Doom), p. 10. See also the fuller discussion of the war in that chapter on Doom.

4. Whether this passage goes back to the time of Isaiah has been debated. Scholars usually agree that much of Isaiah 36–39 was borrowed from 2 Kings to bring the various Isaiah materials together in one place. P. R. Ackroyd points out how Isaiah 38–39 functions in joining First Isaiah with Second Isaiah, "An Interpretation of the Babylonian Exile: A Study of 2 Kings 20, Isaiah 38–39," *SJT* 27 (1974) 329–52.

5. Bright, *Covenant,* 79. Bright does not try to relate the origins of the two covenant traditions, although he does say, "In any event, David's transfer of the Ark to Jerusalem, followed by Solomon's erection of the Temple there, must inevitably have given rise to the belief that Yahweh had chosen Mt. Zion as his abode," ibid., 56.

6. There are differing interpretations of the Davidic covenant. For a careful analysis and judgment on the matter, see Jon D. Levenson, "The Davidic Covenant and Its Modern Interpreters," *CBQ* 41 (1979) 205–19.

7. Bright, *Covenant,* 102.

8. *Ibid.,* 106.

9. Bright admits, "The Zion tradition is assuredly very old" (ibid., 56), and states, "Isaiah's dependence on the Zion traditions is generally recognized" (ibid., 94), but he does not include inviolability in those older traditions.

10. Bright judges that the "fixed dogma" of the inviolability of Zion arose after and as a result of Jerusalem's deliverance from Sennacherib during that Assyrian monarch's second campaign against Hezekiah, ca. 688, *A History of Israel,* 301. This theory of a "second campaign," originally proposed in the nineteenth century, has not had a large following.

11. Bright, *Covenant,* 107.

12. Ibid., 109.

13. The authenticity of the prophecy of a king in chapter 9 has been much debated.

14. Bright, *Covenant*, 109.

15. Ibid.

16. Two volumes, Old Testament Library; Philadelphia: Westminster, 1961 and 1967.

17. Walter Eichrodt, "Prophet and Covenant: Observations on the Exegesis of Isaiah," in *Proclamation and Presence* (FS G. H. Davies; London: SCM, 1970; repr Macon, Georgia: Mercer University, 1983) 167–88.

18. Eichrodt refers to Johnson's *Sacral Kingship in Ancient Israel* (2d ed; Cardiff: University of Wales, 1967) 136ff.

19. Eichrodt, "Prophet," 184.

20. For the various presentations of the idea of covenant in the biblical materials and for the words that, in the views of some scholars, substitute for the word "covenant," see Delbert R. Hillers, *Covenant: The History of a Biblical Idea* (Baltimore: Johns Hopkins, 1969). See also H. Cazelles, "Les structures de la 'beˈrit' dans l'Ancient Testament," *Bulletin du Centre Protestant d'Etudes* 36 (1984) 33–46.

9.

Isaiah: Promise

Isaiah receives a different interpretation from Gerhard von Rad. One of the most renowned and influential Old Testament scholars of the twentieth century, von Rad opened a new direction in the understanding of the prophets of ancient Israel by pointing out that the prophets' task was not to launch out on their own to create a new religion.[1] (Such had been the late nineteenth century interpretation of Israelite prophecy.) Von Rad shows how the prophets reinterpreted and thus revivified the old traditions, for the prophets saw these old traditions as the models on which Yahweh would base his future action.

The election traditions of Israel were the sacral foundations of the people's religious and political existence. In von Rad's view, the vitality of those election traditions had decreased by the time of the classical prophets. The prophets were called to reinterpret, to preach again, and to apply those saving traditions to the new situation of their own day and to the future action of God toward his people. In that future action Yahweh would bring Israel into a new and definitive relationship with himself. Each of the prophets had or developed his own distinctive appropriation and application of the election traditions in order to convey his unique anticipation of that event.

Isaiah is remarkable in many ways, perhaps especially because he is the first prophet who reveals what it means to have grown to maturity in Jerusalem. Von Rad argues that Jerusalem had distinct traditions, independent from the sacred history of Israel. Within the Old Testament, there are three election traditions: the Exodus from Egypt, the founding of Zion, the election

94

of David and his dynasty.[2] The latter two were local traditions of Jerusalem and proper to it. The prophets of the North, namely, Amos and Hosea, show how prophets could use the exodus as the model for God's future action towards his people. Isaiah, however, does not appeal to the exodus tradition. He does not invoke the Pentateuchal traditions at all.[3] Without any reference to the exodus election tradition, Isaiah focuses on the traditions of Zion and of David.[4]

Zion Schema

Jerusalem's city tradition, which Isaiah learned in his youth and appropriated over the years, possessed a set of dramatic scenes which can be reduced to a kind of schema. First, the city is attacked by hostile hordes. These enemy forces do not have a name in the tradition, for they are or represent the threats to the city and to its existence, threats of various kinds that Jerusalem often experienced throughout its existence.

> Ah, the roar of nations,
>   they roar like the roaring of mighty waters!
> The nations roar like the roaring of many waters.
>
> Isa 17:12–13

Although the nations are mythic in nature, each generation knows that those hordes are also symbolic embodiments of the threats against the city in its own particular time.

> He will shake his fist
>   at the mount of the daughter of Zion,
>   the hill of Jerusalem.
>
> Isa 10:32

Second, before the attacking powers accomplish their goal, a mysterious divine action thwarts their advance.

And the multitude of all the nations that fight against Ariel,
    all that fight against her and her stronghold and distress
      her,
shall be like a dream, a vision of the night.

Isa 29:7

The terror that had threatened now disappears. Thus, the third
scene is an enjoyment of deliverance during a reign of peace.

Like birds hovering, so the Lord of hosts
    will protect Jerusalem;
he will protect and deliver it,
    he will spare and rescue it.

Isa 31:5

And they shall beat their swords into plowshares,
    and their spears into pruning hooks;
nation shall not lift up sword against nation,
    neither shall they learn war any more.

Isa 2:4

God's action brings about the time of fulfillment. No more war
threats, no fears of disorder; only peace and fellowship abide.[5]
    The dramatic action of this schema appears also in the
psalms of Zion, Pss 46, 48, and 76.
Scene One:

The nations rage,
    the kingdoms totter.

Psa 46:6

Scene Two:

The kings assembled,
    they came on together.
As soon as they saw it, they were astounded,
    they were in panic, they took to flight.

Psa 48:4–5

Scene Three:

> He makes wars to cease to the end of the earth;
> > he breaks the bow, and shatters the spear,
> > he burns the chariots with fire!
>
> > > Psa 46:9

> There he broke the flashing arrows,
> > the shields, the sword, and the weapons of war.
>
> > > Psa 76:3

The occurrence of this schema in these psalms reveals how important this conception of the miraculous deliverance of the city was for its inhabitants. It is the core of Jerusalem's self-understanding, the symbol against which resonated perhaps any public statement made by a significant citizen of the city. A prophet, especially one like Isaiah who had grown to maturity in Jerusalem, would surely be aware of this symbol's pervasive power.[6]

This schema or drama recurs frequently enough in Isaiah's preaching for us to recognize it as a major element of the prophet's thought. He alludes to it in many different sayings. Depending on whether he emphasizes the attack or the deliverance, he uses the schema both as threat and as promise. On a different occasion, he uses it as a clear prediction of God's future purifying action toward the city. Each different use of the schema displays distinctive elements and features, whether they be theological concerns or literary techniques.

Occurrences

The schema and its elements stand out in dramatic starkness in Isa 17:12–14.

> Ah, the thunder of many peoples,
> > they thunder like the thundering of the sea!

Ah, the roar of nations,
> they roar like the roaring of mighty waters!
The nations roar like the roaring of many waters.

Isa 17:12–13

The hordes lash against the city.

But he will rebuke them, and they will flee away,
> chased like chaff before the wind
> and whirling dust before the storm.

Isa 17:13

God intervenes simply by his rebuke; then peace reigns as the result of this sudden and miraculous intervention by God. The saving of the city establishes the peaceful existence which the city-dwellers greatly desire after the end of all war.

At evening time, behold terror!
> Before morning, they are no more!
This is the portion of those who despoil us,
> and the lot of those who plunder us.

Isa 17:14

This passage presents the schema in a somewhat abrupt form, but this form allows us to see the simplicity of its outline.

This story of Zion's attack is given with geographical detail in Isa 10:27b–34. In this passage the attack is pursued unrelentingly through various locales in a well planned route until the foe "shakes his fist at the mount of the daughter of Zion." A striking feature of this presentation is that the sites named are selected according to the various possibilities for word play on the place names.[7] Eventually, Yahweh intervenes to change this nightmare into the experience of salvation.

Two other appearances of this schema are Isa 29:1–8 and 30:27–33. In the former, Isaiah creatively uses the image of dreaming and waking for the suddenness with which Yahweh will defeat

the multitude of all the nations
　　that fight against Mount Zion.

Isa 29:8

In the latter passage, Isaiah explicitly names Assyria as the foe
that God will defeat

in furious anger and a flame of devouring fire,
　　with cloudburst, tempest and hailstones.

Isa 30:30

Yahweh's Work

Isaiah is so taken by this action of God toward Zion that he
uses special terms to designate God's deliberate strategy. In von
Rad's view, Isaiah begins the use of the term Yahweh's "work"
and "purpose" for this saving act, Yahweh's deliverance of his city
and its people. This salvation, in Isaiah's mind, God proposes for
the immediate future. But although the plan is for something soon
to come, it is not a hasty project. Yahweh deliberates in his council, and the decision is achieved in that setting. This image of a
royal council of God would come readily to Isaiah's mind since his
role as prophet gave him easy access to the king and his council-
ors.[8] This solicitous concern is the way Yahweh relates to the future of his people.

The divine saving action does not leave the people passive but
demands a response of faith and trust.[9] Isaiah often calls this response in faith and trust "looking to" God and his plan. Isaiah
chides the king and the people:

but you did not look to him who did it
　　or have regard for him who planned it long ago.

Isa 22:11

This demand for faith appears most clearly in 7:9b:

If you will not believe,
　　surely you will not be established.

Von Rad proposes that this demand for trust and faith in the God who delivers derives from the Holy War tradition in which Israel was saved only by God's action while, in the meantime, Israel is to look on in faith.[10]

In addition to his use of the Zion tradition to depict God's care of the city, Isaiah used the David tradition to explain part of the salvation that Yahweh was sending his people. Although the prophets did not look upon the kings as models of fidelity to Yahweh, Isaiah could picture the future salvific act of Yahweh as connected with a new scion of the Davidic line. In both Isa 11:1–8 and 9:1b–7 (Hebrew 8:23b–9:6), the prophet predicts a new David.[11] This new occupant of the throne will not be a king who rules on his own power and authority. The promised king will be the vizier of God, one who "is in constant conversation with Yahweh about the government of the world."[12] Isaiah saw beyond his own city and nation.

Salvation

The coming salvation as it applies to Israel will be only partial. Only a remnant will be able to participate in the time of fulfillment, because the people had sinned and only a few are willing to remain true to God. Von Rad points out that this concept does not form an essential and central core for the teaching of Isaiah. Both the idea and the term "remnant" are borrowed from the political realm where it refers to those few who escape the ravages of a war. When Isaiah uses the idea, his use of it is connected with the idea of God's hardening of the people's hearts.

Actually, in Isaiah it is the prophet who hardens the heart in obedience to the command given him by God.

> Make the heart of this people fat,
>   and their ears heavy,
>   and shut their eyes,
> lest they see with their eyes,
>   and hear with their ears

and understand with their hearts,
    and turn, and be healed.

Isa 6:10

The picture of the prophet hardening the hearts of the people has been a problem for theologians who have debated over the meaning of such an action of God. Some have felt that this verse could not have been God's address to the prophet at the beginning of his career, for it would have robbed him of any human motivation. Von Rad points out that Isaiah does not create the idea, but probably chooses this motif from within the prophetic tradition itself. The theme of hardening and blinding appears quite clearly in 1 Kings 22:21, a part of the commissioning of a prophet.[13] This passage forms a close parallel to the call of Isaiah, and this parallel explains how Isaiah was not the first to come up with the idea but rather borrowed from the tradition on this point too.

Hardening Theme

Thus, von Rad disagrees with those who propose for this "hardening task" of the prophet an after-the-fact psychological interpretation, namely, that the continued rejection of the word of God gradually robs one of the capacity to hear and understand it.[14] The text and the tradition behind it are stronger than that. God is depicted as sending an evil spirit or bringing about in some other way a situation that will subvert his own work already in the times of Abimelech (Judg 9:23), of Saul (1 Sam 16:14; 18:10; 19:9), of Absalom (2 Sam 17:14), and of Rehoboam (1 Kings 12:15). Isaiah is caught up in this idea of God sending the effective prophetic word of non-response.

The enigma of obduracy to Yahweh's offer runs through the whole of Isaiah's activity; it is nothing less than the foil which sets off Yahweh's reiterated invitation.[15]

But Yahweh hardens only as a preliminary step toward salvation.

The Future

It is the future which occupies Isaiah most. "Absolutely everything in Isaiah points out into the future."[16] Both the future salvation of Zion, after its scourging purification, and the future new David, elevated above the ordinary kings of Jerusalem, are parts of the coming definitive action of God by which God will raise his people to a new level, a new existence. Thus, Isaiah plays a major role in the prophetic task of calling Israel to a new awareness of God's salvation by invoking the past traditions and making them come alive again.

Isaiah's view of the future is radical both in the sense that he was convinced to the depths of his being that Yahweh was active in his people's life and in the realization that he was acting in a new way. At earlier times, Israel and its leaders would rely on the promises of old to his people. Isaiah thinks back to David:

> O Ariel, Ariel,
>   the city where David encamped!
>
> Isa 29:1

But he also thought of the new David yet to come. Although Isaiah did see judgment coming, he saw beyond it to a rebuilding and to a fulfillment. God had to use his power and authority over all peoples and political forces to bring about the punishment of his own people.

After that disaster, God would bring a new security and peace for his people in Zion and in his land, and then to all people. For Isaiah foresaw that all people would flock to the God who revealed himself on Zion and who would teach those who chose to hear the words of his way.

> It shall come to pass in the latter days
>   that the mountain of the house of the Lord
> shall be established as the highest of the mountains,
>   and shall be raised above the hills;
> and all the nations shall flow to it,
>   and many peoples shall come and say:

"Come, let us go up to the mountain of the Lord,
      to the house of the God of Jacob;
that he may teach us his ways
      and that we may walk in his paths."

Isa 2:2–3

Prophet's Role

Two aspects of von Rad's interpretation of Israelite prophecy remain to be brought into relation to Isaiah. The demands that the role of the prophet made on one called to it gradually became heavier during the period of classical prophecy. This development reaches its peak in Jeremiah and Second Isaiah, where severe suffering is required of the bearer of the word of God. The Servant completes the burdened role of those who must speak for Yahweh.

With Isaiah, the demands are burdensome but not as scarring and prolonged as will be the case with Jeremiah. Isaiah, after all, did have specific periods of activity, perhaps each ending with the expectation that Isaiah's prophetic service had ended. This is certainly the case at the close of his first period, for he writes (or has written) a record of his preaching.

I will bind up the testimony,
      seal the teaching among my disciples,
and will wait for Yahweh,
      who is hiding his face from the house of Jacob,
      and I will hope in him.
Behold, I and the children whom Yahweh has given me
      are signs and portents from Yahweh of hosts,
      who dwells on Mount Zion.

Isa 8:16–18[17]

Isaiah could go on with his life, now that he had completed his task as a prophet. Little did he think the prophetic call would come at least twice again in his life. We do not know how much being a prophet cost Isaiah personally. But that cost seems not to approach the suffering that Jeremiah would endure a century later.

The other aspect of von Rad's distinctive approach to the prophets is their intercessory function. Von Rad sees that the narratives about pre-classical prophecy contain many episodes of intercession (1 Sam 12:19, 23; 15:11). This emphasis on intercession also develops to its fullest in Jeremiah. But even in Isaiah there are texts that can be read in the light of von Rad's hypothesis. Isa 6:11, "How long, O Lord?" is described as an "outburst that comes close to intercession."[18]

Intercession can even accompany thanksgiving, for Isa 12:4 reads,

> Give thanks to the Lord, call upon his name.

Yahweh's characteristic of being open to intercession is clear in Isa 19:22,

> The Lord will smite . . .
>   and he will heed their supplications
>   and heal them.

In Isa 37:2–5, Isaiah is clearly depicted as an intercessor. The king, even after he himself went to the temple, sent messengers to Isaiah to ask him to pray and make intercession for the people in the crisis.

> Lift up your prayer for the remnant that is left.
>   Isa 37:4b

Von Rad did not focus on intercession in his treatment of Isaiah, but these texts show a connection between intercessory prayer and this prophet.

For von Rad, Isaiah is not so much a prophet who intercedes but one who announces God's word about his plan for future action. God will send foreign armies against his city. But for the sake of his promise to David and to his people, Yahweh will deliver those who have trust in him. Yahweh is about to bring Zion into a new relationship with himself by means of his anointed.

Isaiah is a prophet of promise because he relives and revitalizes the promise of old and thus gives the people a new vision and new hope.

Notes

1. Gerhard von Rad, *Old Testament Theology* (2 vols; New York: Harper & Row, 1962, 1965). The second volume, subtitled "The Theology of Israel's Prophetic Traditions," was also published separately as *The Message of the Prophets* (Harper & Row, n.d.). James L. Crenshaw has published an appraisal of von Rad's work: *Gerhard von Rad* (Makers of the Modern Theological Mind; Waco: Word Books, 1978).

2. These were isolated in the dissertation written under von Rad, Edzard Roland, "Die Bedeutung der Erwählungstraditionen für die Eschatologie der alttestamentlichen Propheten" (Heidelberg, 1956).

3. Some twenty passages in Isaiah 1–30 are claimed to refer to the material in the first seven books of the Bible by Seth Erlandsson, *The Burden of Babylon: A Study of Isaiah 13:2–14:23* (Coniectanea Biblica, OT Series 4; Lund: Gleerup, 1970) 119–20, but these passages either are so general that no real connection is evident or are usually judged to be inauthentic.

4. This view, of course, differs from those which stress covenant in Isaiah, covenant as part of the Sinai experience.

5. These are some of the themes that appear in the apocalyptic literature which flourishes some five and a half centuries later. Von Rad never proposed a connection between this city tradition and apocalyptic expression, for he saw the roots of apocalyptic thought to lie in the wisdom tradition. The question whether apocalyptic might be rooted in Canaanite thought was already asked by Hugo Gressmann at the turn of the twentieth century and answered in the affirmative in his *Der Ursprung der israelitisch-jüdischen Eschatologie* (Göttingen: Vandenhoeck und Ruprecht, 1905). Much depends on the dating of the Zion Psalms; for a post-exilic dating of these psalms see Gunther

Wanke, *Die Zionstheologie der Korachiten in ihren Traditions-geschichtlichen Zusammenhang* (BZAW 97; Berlin: Alfred Töpelmann, 1966).

6. Perhaps something comparable in the United States would be a reference to the Star-Spangled Banner or Lincoln's Gettysburg Address.

7. In Micah 1:10–12 we have the same literary feature, a march that advances according to a path of puns. Von Rad does not comment on it, but some scholars have given examples of the effect by translating this passage and keeping the puns (Bernhard Duhm, *Das Buch Jesaja* [5th ed.; Göttingen: Vandenhoeck & Ruprecht, 1968] 103), or creating an invasion of their own country on the same principle (Luis Alonso-Schökel, "Is. 10, 28–32, Análisis estilistico," *Biblica* 40 [1959] 230–36) or simply punning on place names at random (Paul Auvray, *Isaïe 1–39* [Sources Bibliques; Paris: Gabalda, 1972] 139).

8. There have been many studies on the idea of the prophet entering the heavenly court. For a survey of studies, a survey that also includes comparative materials, see Max Polley, "Hebrew Prophecy within the Council of Yahweh, Examined in its Ancient Near Eastern Setting," in *Scripture in Context: Essays on the Comparative Method* (Pittsburgh Theological Monograph Series 34; Pittsburgh: Pickwick, 1980) 141–56.

9. At least one scholar has gone further and suggested a quietist strain in Isaiah: C.-A. Keller, "Das quietische Element in der Botschaft des Jesaja," *TZ* 11 (1955) 81–97.

10. This, then, would be an influence on the city tradition of Zion from the people tradition of Israel.

11. For a fuller discussion of these passages, see the previous chapter on covenant.

12. *Old Testament Theology,* 2:172–73.

13. One should also keep in mind that the literary influence might have gone in the other direction.

14. Von Rad's German is striking: "Das Nichtwollen wird mit dem Nichtkönnen bestraft," *Die Botschaft der Propheten* (Munich: Siebenstern Taschenbuch, 1967) 119.

15. *Theology,* 2:154.

16. Ibid., 2:155.

17. This is von Rad's rendering. He begins by reading the verb as first person singular, "I will bind up," rather than the imperative, "Bind up."

18. On this idea, see Arnold B. Rhodes, "Israel's Prophets as Intercessors," in *Scripture in History & Theology* (FS J. Coert Rylaarsdam; Pittsburgh Theological Monograph Series 17; Pittsburgh: Pickwick, 1977) 107–28. And for a critique of this emphasis, see Samuel E. Balentine, "The Prophet as Intercessor: A Reassessment," *JBL* 103 (1984) 161–73.

10

Isaiah: Purification

Isaiah is a prophet who preaches a coming purification of the city of Jerusalem. Hermann Barth offers this interpretation of the prophetic activity of Isaiah in a study which investigates the development of the Isaiah tradition.[1] Barth's analysis concludes that there was a major revision of the collected words of Isaiah at the time of king Josiah in the late seventh century and that the current book of Isaiah should be read with full awareness of that editorial work.[2]

Isaiah saw that Jerusalem was not serving Yahweh with the completeness and fidelity that he demanded. The religious fervor was weak, the social conscience weaker still. The people forgot that God demands much from those whom he chooses. Zion could not simply rest content in the knowledge of her election.

> For Jerusalem has stumbled,
>   and Judah has fallen;
> because their speech and their deeds are against the Lord,
>   defying his glorious presence.
>
> Isa 3:8

Prophetic Plea

Isaiah had hoped for a response of trust and reliance on the God who spoke to his people through Isaiah's own prophetic activity. Yahweh had sent prophets in order to accomplish his purposes. Isaiah, no doubt, saw himself in a line of prophets. God now was appealing to his people through a new prophet, and God was awaiting their answer. However, they were "a rebellious people, lying sons who will not hear the instruction of the Lord" (30:9). They should trust Yahweh and his word, but they despise this word, and trust in oppression and perverseness (30:12).

They have failed to understand the sequence of disasters that God had sent them (9:8–21; Hebrew 9:7–20).[3] They have fulfilled the words of Isaiah's commission:

> Make the heart of this people fat,
>   and their ears heavy,
>   and shut their eyes;
> lest they see with their eyes,
>   and hear with their ears,
> and understand with their hearts,
>   and turn and be healed.
>
> Isa 6:10

It is a fairly clear case of prediction and fulfillment.

Yahweh certainly had every right to abandon this people (2:6). Surely his patience was long-suffering enough. No god was expected to stretch out his hands to people oblivious of their obligation to respond to the God who calls. No wonder that Isaiah decided to end his prophetic ministry. Henceforth he would leave Jerusalem to the treatment she deserved from her God.

Cleansing

But Isaiah's experience of Yahweh was more complicated than just seeing him as a purely judgmental God. Yahweh had to punish the people because of their sins, but his choice was to use that punishment not simply to penalize the people but to draw them closer to himself. He could not simply abandon mercy in order to pursue justice. He would purify his people in Jerusalem and let them have another chance. The chastisement that would come to them would cause them to become more faithful to him.

A clear example of this desire of Yahweh to cleanse Jerusalem appears in Isa 29:1–7. Here the prophet depicts hostile armies attacking Jerusalem. In their vanguard is Yahweh!

> I will distress Ariel,
>   and there shall be moaning and lamentation,
>   and she shall be to me like an Ariel.
> And I will encamp against you round about,
>   and will besiege you with towers
>   and I will raise siegeworks against you.
>
>   Isa 29:2–3

God brings the attackers to purge Jerusalem. Barth explains that Isaiah is thinking of the Assyrians in this passage, even though he does not name them. He omits any name, because the long-standing and well-known tradition left the attackers unnamed.

Barth's interpretation of 29:5a differs from the RSV, and that difference is crucial in understanding the message of Isaiah. In the reading of the RSV: Jerusalem is attacked, and Yahweh delivers her. The deliverance reads:

> But the multitude of your foes shall be like small dust,
>   and the multitude of the ruthless like passing chaff.
> And in an instant, suddenly,
>   you will be visited by the Lord of hosts . . .
>
>   Isa 29:5–6

The RSV's note on "your foes," however, admits that that translation is a conjecture. The current Hebrew text reads "your strangers." The Dead Sea Scrolls' copy of Isaiah reads "your haughty ones." This seems the original reading.[4] In this way, Yahweh brings the peoples against Jerusalem to rid her of the haughty ones and the ruthless ones that are *within her.* Yahweh's prophet speaks words of judgment, punishment, and purification. But the final goal is salvation.

This alternation of woe and weal, of threat and promise, occurs elsewhere in the authentic words of Isaiah: 1:21–26, 10:33a + 11:1–5, 28:14–16, 31:1–4 + 8a.[5] Some critical scholars have had difficulty in seeing a prophet uttering a threat one minute and then following the threat immediately with a promise. This behavior, for them, is too unstable and erratic a way for a prophet of God to act. But such a change in mood is not a real problem from this perspective. God is sending punishment in order to effect a purification. Salvation must be preceded, in the setting of sin, by punishment.

Barth allows that Isaiah lived in a city whose tradition proclaimed the inviolability of the city—the city could not be taken, for it was the dwelling place of God. But Barth does not think that Isaiah simply repeated that idea. God's plan, as a result of the sin of the people, was to cleanse the city, to effect a new and faithful Jerusalem. This promise of a new Jerusalem is contained in 28:16,

> Thus says the Lord God,
> "Behold, I am laying in Zion for a foundation
>   a stone, a tested stone,
> a precious cornerstone, of a sure foundation:
>   'He who believes will not be in haste.' "

This cornerstone is the foundation of the *new* Jerusalem.[6]

Isaiah Reinterpreted

Barth thinks that the authentic preaching of Isaiah was not passed on to others without reflection. He proposes that the Isaiah tradition was transmitted among people who understood that the words of the prophet were important and meaningful for their own day. They found them applicable to daily events, or they made them that way. Thus, about a century after the lifetime and activity of Isaiah his sayings produced new resonances among those who treasured them.

At the time of Josiah, according to the Deuteronomist's report, the king of Jerusalem had plans to cleanse the religious practice in Jerusalem, and presumably to restore his realm to its Davidic splendor and purity.[7] Thus, Josiah centralized all sacrificial worship of Yahweh in Jerusalem. He purged the cult of its non-Yahwistic elements and established a law code as the model of his reform. This reformed pure Yahwistic worship had political implications as well. Just as the Yahweh-worshiper David built a politically independent empire, so might Judah now regain the northern areas and begin to restore the Davidic establishment.

This time of religious and political fervor inspired a radical reediting of the book of Isaiah.[8] The thrust of this reworking of the Isaiah tradition was to show that Yahweh was about to crush Assyria in its own land. Judah would witness its own rebirth at the demise of Assyria. The strength of this conviction was enough to change Isaiah's qualified hope—that Jerusalem would survive the severe chastisement and purification it was about to undergo—into a firm and unnuanced conviction that Jerusalem would not be taken by the army of any enemy. In the minds of the editors of this new version of Isaiah, God gave his unqualified support to the city of his election.

Barth sees the prophet Isaiah as one who believed in a perceptive and precise theology: Yahweh had to punish his people, but after the punishment he would bring about a new order of things. For example,

> The wolf shall dwell with the lamb,
>   and the leopard shall lie down with the kid,
> and the calf and the lion and the fatling together,
>   and a little child shall lead them.
>
> Isa 11:6

Persons of later generations in their own times may have read such words of Isaiah with simplistic connotations of unconditional protection and lived their lives according to different implications. But the careful reader can filter out the original intent of Isaiah himself.

Chapter 1 as Summary

The major idea of Barth on Isaiah has been applied by R. E. Clements in his commentary on Isaiah 1–39.[9] There was a major editorial reorientation at the time of Josiah. Clements points out that Chapter 1 stands as a summary of the preaching of Isaiah.[10] It reflects the perspective and goal of Isaiah's whole prophetic enterprise. Isa 1:2–26 is a selection of sayings of the prophet which were brought together as a preface to his collected words.

The structure of the passage is this: vv 2–3, nature and extent of Israel's sin; vv 3–9, judgment of God upon this sin; vv 10–17, way of deliverance from sin; vv 18–20, appeal for repentance and a return to obedience; vv 21–26, hope of a purifying judgment and restoration. The remaining five verses of the chapter are editorial expansions and generalizations that were appended after these authentic sayings were brought together.[11]

Clements stresses that Isaiah, although a citizen of Jerusalem and familiar with its traditions, was concerned not simply about the holy city. His thought always dealt with the people of God as a whole—not with just Jerusalem or only Judah, but with the totality of Israel, aside from the division into the two kingdoms and aside from the later loss of political independence for the North.[12]

All Israel

An example of this unified thinking about Israel is 9:2–7 (Hebrew 9:1–6). Although many scholars have dated this passage to a later time, Clements defends its Isaianic authorship.[13] The historical note in 9:1 refers to the severe treatment of the northern area by Tiglath-Pileser in 733, splitting it into three Assyrian provinces.[14] The prophecy of 9:2–7, in the form of a royal accession oracle, was altered when Hezekiah came to the throne. The hope was high that he would restore the throne of Jerusalem as the center of an empire that would equal if not surpass that of David.[15]

This hope for the future of Israel did not rest on any tradition of the inviolability of the city. Clements does not agree with those scholars who see this tradition of the city's divine election and protection as constitutive of the Jerusalem mentality during the length of the monarchy there.[16] Clements's assessment is that this tradition of inviolability of the city developed during the seventh century and came to its height at the time of Josiah, who used it as part of his program of reform and renewal. The miraculous defense of the city is a late monarchic development rather than an inheritance from the Canaanites. Thus, the preaching of Isaiah was concerned with bringing the people back to God. Israel had gone astray, breaking fidelity with Yahweh by worshiping other gods and by putting more faith in its own political planning than in its God. Isaiah saw that such planning was misled and could result in nothing good. But more important was his desire to awaken people to their own religious infidelity, so that the coming purification of the people would bring about a time of greater service to God. The success of the purifying work of God depended on the response of the people.

Notes

1. Hermann Barth, *Die Jesaja-Worte in der Josiazeit: Israel und Assur als Thema einer produktiven Neuinterpretation der Jesajaüberlieferung* (WMANT 48; Neukirchen-Vluyn: Neukirchener, 1977). This volume is a reworking of his dissertation, *Israel und das Assyrerreich in den nichtjesajanischen Texten des Protojesajabuches* (Hamburg, 1974).

2. Vermeylen (chapter on Doom above) also proposes that there was a revision of the Isaiah collection at this time, but does not see quite as much editorial activity as Barth for that particular time. In some respects, the Norwegian scholar Sigmund Mowinckel was a predecessor of both Vermeylen and Barth with his article, "Die Komposition des Jesajabuches, Kap. 1–39," *Acta Orientalia* 11 (1933) 267–92.

3. Many commentators view the list in this way: (1) the Philistine and Aramean wars against Israel, 9:7–10, (2) the revolution of Jehu, 9:12–16, (3) civil war in the Northern Kingdom, 9:16–20. And some commentators add two further disasters from chapter 5: (4) earthquake, 5:25, and (5) invasion, 5:26–29. See, for example, Otto Kaiser, *Isaiah 1–12* (1st ed, OTL; Philadelphia: Westminster, 1972) 133–39. In his second English edition (Westminster, 1983) 223–24, Kaiser even rearranges the sequence to get what he perceives as the right historical flow.

4. Barth, *Die Jesaja-Worte*, 185–86. Barth points out that R. Lowth in 1780 had already suggested this reading. In some Hebrew scripts the "r" and the "d" resemble each other very much, and this interchange of letters accounts for the differences. I.e., the Dead Sea Scroll copy has the "d" while the current Hebrew has "r."

5. Joseph Jensen, "Weal and Woe in Isaiah," *CBQ* 43 (1981) 167–87, has shown that sometimes the picture of what should and can be is presented before the threats are given to the people who do not respond to God. This order is precisely the case in 2:2–4 and 2:6–21. Jensen stresses, among other points, that this was a unique style of pedagogy of Isaiah (or perhaps an editor) in which the future was envisioned before the present was critiqued.

6. Barth, *Die Jesaja-Worte*, p. 12.

7. On the hopes and activity of Josiah, see Bustenay Oded, "Josiah and the Deuteronomic Reform," in John H. Hayes and J. Maxwell Miller, eds., *Israelite and Judean History* (OTL; Philadelphia: Westminster, 1977) 458–69.

8. G. Sheppard adopts Barth's proposal and shows how influential that redaction was on the subsequent growth of the entire book of Isaiah. Gerald T. Sheppard, "The Anti-Assyrian Redaction and the Canonical Context of Isaiah 1–39," *JBL* 104 (1985) 193–216.

9. R. E. Clements, *Isaiah 1–39* (NCB; Grand Rapids: Eerdmans, 1980). Clements also mentions the influence of Barth on his thinking in *Isaiah and the Deliverance of Jerusalem* (JSOTSS 13; Sheffield: JSOT, 1980).

10. See G. Fohrer, "Jesaja 1 als Zusammenfassung der Verkündigung Jesajas," *ZAW* 74 (1962) 251–68; repr in BZAW 99 (1967) 148–66.

11. One might think that 1:27a, "Zion shall be redeemed by justice," is such a clear enunciation of the idea of purification that it would be difficult to deny the words to Isaiah. But both Clements, *Isaiah 1–39*, 37, and Barth, *Die Jesaja-Worte*, 292–94, point out that the whole saying, i.e., 1:27–28, which includes the destroying of rebels and sinners and the consumption of those who forsake the Lord, suggests a post-exilic time and the struggles of the restoration.

12. This is somewhat a deviation from the majority of commentators on Isaiah who stress the dominance of Jerusalem over the thought of the prophet Isaiah.

13. Some scholars who accept Isaianic authenticity, as Bright and von Rad (see chapters on Covenant and Promise above), understand this oracle to refer to a future king, not a reigning king or one in the process of ascending the throne.

14. The three were Magidu (Megiddo), Gal'azu (Gilead), and Dor (on the coast).

15. For the shock that was caused by the collapse of his program, see Stanley Brice Frost, "The Death of Josiah: A Conspiracy of Silence," *JBL* 87 (1968) 369–82.

16. Here, of course, Clements parts company with Barth.

11.

Composition, Redaction, Context

For many critical scholars, the great variety of ideas in Isaiah 1–39 precludes the possibility that one person spoke such differing and contradictory words. Some scholars say that, no matter how long a person may live and how many different situations that person might experience, no public speaker would have uttered such contrary and seemingly incompatible statements as are contained in the collected words of our prophets. But even apart from that extreme statement, it is inevitable that if we read the Bible carefully, we are led to admit that the present text of the book of Isaiah, even the section 1–39 by itself, contains many words beyond those of the prophet Isaiah.

As seen earlier, the prophet himself probably did not write his own words.[1] The prophet's words were collected by those who heard him and were struck by his words. The number or percentage of the words of the prophet that were striking enough to be reduced to writing will never be known. Tradition simply passed on what seemed significant in each era.

Collections

The theories on the origin of the first book of Isaiah generally fall into two groups: those which propose that the Isaiah tradition began simply in one collection which grew dramatically and drastically and those which conclude that several independent collections existed which were later united after each had its own independent existence and growth.[2]

Bernhard Duhm can be taken as an exponent of the position that the book of Isaiah began in a combination of several booklets which were brought together at a rather late date.[3] The various pieces were brought together with little thought of forming a unity and simply out of the desire to bring together those things that remain from Isaiah.

Sigmund Mowinckel is representative of those who imagine a more unitive growth to the Isaiah material.[4] For Mowinckel, the book of Isaiah begins with the memoirs of the prophet. Then various efforts were made to enhance and update the sayings of the prophet. This approach allows for the organic growth of the tradition. This view of Isaiah is part of a general approach to the biblical tradition which sees the tradition as a whole, and even the tradition of a single preacher within ancient Israel, as a vital and living entity, not a passive collection, something that was only acted upon.

Editions

More recent study on the sayings of Isaiah emphasize the process of editing more than the process of collecting and treasuring the words of the prophet. The sayings of Isaiah formed a significant document which scribes and scholars copied not only to preserve and protect for a future generation but especially to give their contemporaries fresh insight and helpful explanations to enable them to see the meaning of things and events in their own day.

Hermann Barth's idea that the first major reworking of the collection of Isaiah occurred during the reign of Josiah stresses a creative kind of editing.[5] The threat that Assyria would take over the city and the land had grown somewhat, but at the time of Josiah the threat could be ignored because Yahweh was promising, by means of the new interpretations of the words of Isaiah, a new deliverance for his people. Assyria would be defeated in its own land, and the new God-given leader would lead the people to a new order of social existence. This deliberate revision of the words of Isaiah was occasioned by the new political and religious atmosphere.

J. Vermeylen sees more frequent editorial work on the collection. He proposes that the whole collection was reworked from a new perspective about every fifty years from the time of Isaiah on.[6] Later in its growth, the editing was made by way of addition, since the text had already become too sacred to tamper with in any major way. These new editions began with a version in the time of Manasseh, a version which redirected Isaiah's threats which had been given against the northern kingdom (which now had fallen) to the southern kingdom as well. At the time of Josiah there occurred an edition which added the Messianic passages. That redaction was followed by two deuteronomic revisions. Finally the post-restoration struggles after the exile led to various additions.

Isaiah 1–66

Thus far, the discussion about the growth of the Isaiah material considered only Isaiah 1–39.[7] But Isaiah, as he was known for at least sixteen centuries (and is still known by those who do not accept a historical-critical approach to the Bible), appears in all the words of all sixty-six chapters in the book of Isaiah. Even Jesus in the gospels refers to material Isa 40–66 simply as Isaiah.[8] Whatever are the real words of the real Isaiah now, the complete book of Isaiah is where one finds the words of Isaiah. And this book may be the appropriate setting to hear and ponder the eighth century prophet.

Various contemporary scholars have recently emphasized the need to interpret any part of the Bible within the context of the whole Bible. This development is perhaps different from the saying from the Reformation that the Bible is its own best interpreter.[9] The saying at that time may have had more a Christological thrust than it does now. Scholars today often have additional focuses.

One might look for the literary unity that the final editor saw in or gave to the book. This would be somewhat comparable to those who would study the epics of Homer to see the meaning of the current form of that tradition rather than the various developments of the tradition.[10] Thus, the present literary whole is the matter to be analyzed. Others prefer to think of the theological unity that the Bible possesses in its quality of being the word of God. The Bible would be read and studied as sacred and normative. That is, the canon (all the books regarded as Scripture) is the determining factor for interpreting the Bible. Still other scholars might want to emphasize more the historical or the sociological factors in the development of the text.

Many proposals have been made for Isaiah and for the context against which to interpret the prophet. Perhaps one need not decide at the outset that there is only one correct way of seeing the matter or of reading scripture. There may, in fact, be several important voices speaking in scripture, and perhaps none of them should be silenced. Debate occasionally arises over the question which voice should be listened to.

Symbols and Structure

If one takes the whole of Isaiah 1–66 as a unit and looks to the underlying themes and structures, purposes and statements, then certain unifying factors and elements take on special significance. Rémi Lack brings out these deep-rooted structures in his study of the symbolism of the book.[11] Lack analyzes each section of the book to find the dominant images and to see the relationships among them.

The first section (1:2–5:24) announces judgment and has three major groups of images: urban (especially maternal),[12] rural (vegetation), and the interplay between the city (Jerusalem) and the country (Judah), with the city being the center. The second section (5:25–9:6) brings that judgment into reality under the images of flood and military disaster. The third section (9:7–11:16) carries forward the symbolism of vegetation and the seasons, and it includes the motifs of food and trees. The fourth section (13:1–35:10), the largest one within 1–39, contains the sounds of war, the vision of flood, and aspects of a hurricane.

Many of these themes and symbols of 1–39 reappear in 40–55. Prominent in this next section are the alternation between the rainy season and the dry summer, the situation of space and time, and the symbol of Zion as mother. Chapters 56–66 show their own symmetrical structure. The whole book, however, is held together, because it was so edited, by three eschatological themes: the holy mountain, the fertility of Zion, and the revelation of the divine glory.

Lack shows the literary structure that underlies the book of Isaiah. He claims that this structural unity is operative even if the writers and editors of the school of Isaiah, which passed on the words of the prophet and of his followers, did not intentionally put that unity and structure in the various parts. The work as it stands now speaks through the structures that reside in the text.

Connecting Hinge

A very different attempt to see the relation of 1–39 to 40–66 appears from the pen of P. R. Ackroyd.[13] He starts with chapters 38–39, which Lack considers simply part of an appendix to 1–35. Chapters 38–39 may be out of chronological order (happening before the events of 36–37), but that possibility emphasizes the role they play in the literary structure. Chapter 38 (the Babylonian ambassadors who see all that the king and people have) and chapter 39 (the sickness and recovery of Hezekiah) do not simply succeed in bringing all of the Isaiah material together and in ending the collection. They also function structurally.

These two chapters tie 1–35 to 40–55, for they show that the exile was forewarned, but that it also was—or could have been—seen, even during the course of the exile itself, as a temporary situation, a time of stress and discomfort, which could pass if the proper repentance would be produced. The editorial work not only began the gradual enhancement of the figure of Hezekiah in the tradition, but it especially prepared the reader for the reality of the exile and the cure that the writers saw as possible, based on the events of the past. The work of the editors shaped the message of the book for all time.

Canonical Relation

Because Scripture comes to the believing interpreter as a whole, as a canon of inspired sacred books, the interpreter must base the interpretation on the text as it stands, and not on how one might reconstruct it. Brevard Childs insists that the divisions that have been discovered within the book of Isaiah have led interpreters to be content with the theology of each section of the book rather than to seek the meaning of the whole in the canonical form of the tradition.[14] Surely the Bible does not ask one to read Isaiah 1–39 as a different book from 40–55 and 56–66. Rather, the book of Isaiah is the unit for interpretation.

The relation between First Isaiah and Second Isaiah can be seen in Childs's understanding of the phrases, the "former things" and the "latter things," in Second Isaiah.[15] These expressions that occur several times in Second Isaiah refer, for Childs, to the prophecies of First Isaiah over against those of Second Isaiah. The promises of Isa 40–55 are clearly the completion of the judgment threatened in 1–39. All those things that Isaiah of Jerusalem and his collection spoke of came true by the time of or in the preaching of Isaiah of Babylon. The canonical shape of the book is vindicated by this relation between the two parts, the "former things" balancing the "latter things." Third Isaiah simply carries the work of Second Isaiah one step further.[16]

Cultic Prophecy

The continuity between First, Second, and Third Isaiah is seen by John Eaton to lie in the character of the group which passed on and added to the oracles of the original prophet.[17] Isaiah himself was a cultic prophet whose career began in the scene where Yahweh is manifested as King on Zion in the Jerusalem temple (chapter 6). Eaton here builds on Scandinavian scholarship which has emphasized the cultic activity of prophets. Within organized worship itself, the prophet, in this case Isaiah, spoke (from the side of God, as it were) to the assembled worshiping community at the festivals. Conversely, he also spoke for the people in their response and address to God.

Isaiah's disciples handed on the prophet's words and also continued his activity of prophecy within the cult. Even after this group went to Babylon and was without the temple, its members continued to experience in memory and imagination the festival rites and actions. They, too, could speak now the words of God and now the words of his people. God's marriage to Zion, an image Isaiah used in the parable of the vineyard (chapter 5), is part of the imagery that reappears in the prophecies uttered within the same cultic-prophetic school of Isaiah.

In this way, not only is 40–55 linked to the prophet Isaiah, but also many later passages (e.g., 13–14, 24–27, 33) share in the ideas and buoyancy within that prophet-cult tradition. The elements of continuing cult prophecy that Eaton identifies throughout the sections of Isaiah are (1) the liturgical assertion of Yahweh's supremacy, (2) God's speeches and dialogues before the congregation, and (3) liturgical declaration of royal destiny. The book of Isaiah is the deposit of a continuing group who carried on the work and role of Isaiah.

Deliberate Connection

R. E. Clements, too, has sought the living connection between the two major parts of the book of Isaiah.[18] For him no chance arrangement, nor economic consideration (to make good use of the remainder of the scroll on which Isaiah 1–39 had already been written)[19] explains the placing of 40–55 after 1–39. Nor does Clements see a "school of the prophet Isaiah," as several other scholars have seen.[20] Rather, themes and ideas unite the parts. The concerns for Jerusalem and for the Davidic line, expressed in 1–39 in the form of judgments, find their resolution in 40–55. With the logic and comprehensiveness of the faith of Israel, the editors saw that the two parts went together.

Indeed, this connection may have come from a historical connection as well as from a theological one. Clements underscores the continued use of the images of blindness and deafness for the erring people, images that Isaiah first used in his call narrative (chapter 6). Those images recur, for example, in the promises of

40–55 and in those previous passages which may come from that prophet's time. "The eyes of the blind shall be opened, and the ears of the deaf unstopped" (35:5). "Bring forth the people who are blind, yet have eyes, who are deaf, yet have ears!" (43:8). The prophet of the exile could well have mulled over the call of Isaiah, his words and his images, for his preaching serves as the complement to those of his predecessor.

Social Dynamic

One aspect of the relationship among the parts of the book of Isaiah has been neglected thus far. Modern biblical scholarship has always looked for the original social setting to understand biblical texts. More recently the dynamic social structures and movements have been sought to clarify the context of biblical thought and experience. Walter Brueggemann presents his proposals for First, Second, and Third Isaiah.[21]

For Brueggemann, the literary relations among the parts of the book do not tell the full story. Nor is he content to say simply that the canon gives us the book of Isaiah as judgment and promise. His analysis of the times and social conditions of the prophetic voices results in this proposal. First Isaiah offers social criticism, a critique of a society and its ideology. It is a prophetic judgment as it stands in relation to the book as a whole. Second Isaiah, coming after the fall of Jerusalem, argues for an embrace of pain as a public action as a way eventually to achieve hope. Third Isaiah, so often ignored in this discussion as a separate voice within the Isaiah tradition, brings a release of social imagination. The community can think thoughts of hope (not other-worldly dreams) in the new post-exilic situation.

Brueggemann tries to show that the biblical message is not something static in its origins or in itself. The book of Isaiah, then, exhibits that social dynamic that ancient Israel experienced at specific times and expressed in its literature.

Unitary Editing

A recent proposal to explain the unity in the book of Isaiah, whether to discover its total message or to discern the literary process which formed it, focuses on the verbal connections as keys to the editorial process. Rolf Rendtorff confirms the threefold division of the book.[22] He finds that there is clear evidence that an individual or a group edited the entire book from one perspective. The various parts have been placed quite carefully and with a conscious effort to obtain the desired effect.

The central section, 40–55, is also central to the editorial activity. That section governs the whole in its imagery, even using that imagery in the editorial additions that appear in other parts of the book. Thus, the ideas of "guilt," "trust," and "glory," found in the first chapter of 40–55 reappear in the crucial chapters of the other parts of the book, namely, 1, 12, 59, and 66. Other major items of editorial unity are "Zion," "remaining," "holy One of Israel," and "righteousness." Often each section keeps to a particular understanding of the common term, while the term appears in a different light in some other part of the book. The editing of Isaiah was a conscious activity, not something that simply developed without organization or plan.

All these recent attempts to see the process by which the book came into existence try to balance out an older approach. That older approach was to discard as unimportant and inferior those words which did not come from the prophet himself. Some forms of scholarship were interested in the prophet himself and his message. Today, Isaiah stands as a summit of prophecy, but scholars also want to see how his words come to us and how those words generated other words.

Notes

1. This view of a prophet has been presented persuasively for the prophet Amos by Robert B. Coote in his *Amos Among the Prophets: Composition and Theology* (Philadelphia: Fortress, 1981).

2. This division is found in Otto Eissfeldt, *The Old Testa-*

ment: An Interpretation (New York: Harper and Row, 1965) 306. Eight different explanations of the composition of 1–39 are reviewed by Seth Erlandsson, *The Burden of Babylon*, 48–54.

3. Bernhard Duhm, *Das Buch Jesaja* (4th ed, Göttingen, 1922).

4. Sigmund Mowinckel, *Jesaja Disiplene: Profetien fra Jesaja til Jeremia* (Oslo, 1926); idem, "Die Komposition des Jesajabuches, Kap. 1–39," *Acta Orientalia* 11 (1933) 267–92.

5. Hermann Barth, see the chapter on Purification above.

6. J. Vermeylen, see the chapter on Doom above.

7. Vermeylen, however, also studies the structure of the whole book. He sees, for example, that each of the major sections of the book of Isaiah ends with a reference to the return of exiles: 11:11–16; 27:12–13; 35:8–10; 56:8; 66:20.

8. John 1:23, referring to Isa 40:3. The evangelists themselves more frequently refer quotations from Isa 40–66 to simply "the prophet Isaiah."

9. "Scriptura scripturae interpres," Martin Luther, quoted by Robert M. Grant, *A Short History of the Interpretation of the Bible* (rev. ed., pb; New York: Macmillan, 1963) 133. Grant refers this dictum to the desire to be independent of patristic commentary, but the idea itself goes back to the patristic period, to Tertullian and Origen and the arguments against the Marcionites, who wanted Christians to rid themselves of the Hebrew Scriptures.

10. The same thing might be said of the Gilgamesh tradition; again, see Tigay, *The Evolution of the Gilgamesh Epic*.

11. Rémi Lack, *La Symbolique du Livre d'Isaïe: Essai sur l'image littéraire comme élément de structuration* (AnBib 59; Rome: Biblical Institute, 1973).

12. On the city as mother, see John J. Schmitt, "The Motherhood of God and Zion as Mother," *Revue Biblique* 92 (1985) 557–69.

13. Peter R. Ackroyd, "An Interpretation of the Babylonian Exile: A Study of 2 Kings 20, Isaiah 38–39," *SJT* 27 (1974) 329–52.

14. Brevard Childs, *Introduction to the Old Testament as Scripture* (Philadelphia: Fortress Press, 1979) 311–38.

15. Cf. C. R. North, "The Former Things and the New Things in Deutero-Isaiah," in *Studies in Old Testament Prophecy* (FS Theodore H. Robinson; Edinburgh: T. & T. Clark, 1957) 111–26, and A. Schoors, "Les choses antérieures et les choses nouvelles dans les oracles deutéro-isaïens," *ETL* 40 (1964) 19–47.

16. Sheppard shows how one particular redaction in the developing tradition might influence the whole of the canonical book, cf. the already cited Sheppard, "The Anti-Assyrian Redaction," *JBL* 104 (1985) 193–216.

17. John Eaton, "The Isaiah Tradition," in *Israel's Prophetic Tradition* (FS Peter R. Ackroyd; Cambridge: Cambridge University, 1982) 58–76.

18. R. E. Clements, "The Unity of the Book of Isaiah," *Interpretation* 36 (1982) 117–29.

19. This is the position of Robert H. Pfeiffer, *Introduction to the Old Testament* (New York: Harper & Brothers, 1948) 447–48. He dates this joining of 40–66 to 1–39 about 200 BCE.

20. Scandinavian and British scholars have argued strongly for this position. Some other scholars just as vigorously deny it; e.g., Vermeylen, *Du prophète*.

21. Walter Brueggemann, "Unity and Dynamics in the Isaiah Tradition," *JSOT* 29 (1984) 89–107.

22. Rolf Rendtorff, "Zur Komposition des Buches Jesaja," *VT* 34 (1984) 295–320.

12.

Isaiah and the Believer

The preceding review allows one to see the great variety of thought within the book of Isaiah. The book stands as a monument of religious experience of ancient Israel through many different ages. It is a witness to the vitality and intensity of the belief of Israelites over generations.

The search for the original Isaiah has helped to point out that a complex variety of religious experience is present even at the earliest levels of this book. These different voices, these different religious perceptions, all speak to the believer today. Faith—unless it consists simply in a static grip on a doctrine—is willing, indeed needs, to see the complexity of life and especially of the religious commitment in a complicated world. The book of Isaiah throbs with the variety and many-faceted reality of life.

One need not choose among the interpretations of Isaiah as the final meaning of the book. That approach might stifle the Spirit who can be found in all the words. Any interpretation that attempts to see a monolithic meaning in the entire book of Isaiah would do violence to the text of the book and the history of its appropriation. We should try to hear all the voices of Scripture.

This thought recalls a discussion in a class where the author was the teacher. It was a small class, and the discussion was freewheeling. One student got to the point of saying that she wanted Scripture to be all things to all people, to soothe the heart of the troubled, to strengthen the resolve of the committed, to bring joy and hope to sinner and saint alike. A fellow student gasped. For him Scripture had but one meaning, and it was the student's task to find that one meaning. The wobbly attitude of his classmate shocked him. The two approaches are certainly different.

I must side with the student who could hear numerous voices and messages in Scripture. There are loud ones and soft ones, and we hear them differently on our different days. Surely God's Word is not a booming sound with no subtle overtones or echoes or even different resonances within it. Let us hear it all.

I suspect that Isaiah would want his message and his book to be heard in their fullness. He would not want any of the threat to be missed, nor would he want the wisdom neglected. He wants us to be converted to the God of the covenant who gives many promises to his people. He knows that we all need purification before we reach the wholeness and holiness that God wills for us.

Index of Persons

130

Index of Scriptural Passages